CURRENT CRITICISM

Essays from Speaker and Gavel

ROBERT O. WEISS   BERNARD L. BROCK
Editors

Published by Delta Sigma Rho—Tau Kappa Alpha
1971

Library of Congress Catalogue Card No. 77-171429
Copyright 1971 Delta Sigma Rho–Tau Kappa Alpha

Published by Delta Sigma Rho–Tau Kappa Alpha, Theodore J. Walwik, National
Secretary, Department of Speech and Theatre, Slippery Rock State College,
Slippery Rock, Pennsylvania 16057

Printed at the Allen Press, Inc., Lawrence, Kansas 66044

Cover design by Garret Boone

PREFACE

This volume of current rhetorical criticism is addressed firstly to those who see the analysis and evaluation of public discourse as desirable and want to join in the venture of producing it. We are hopeful that the essays gathered together in this book may serve a generative function, that they may stand as models and suggestions of what can be done. Substantially more criticism of this kind is needed, we feel. Therefore, if these studies prove to be useful and provocative, readers may be encouraged to produce their own, whether for their own purposes or for public consumption in the classroom, the press, or the professional journal.

The function of criticism is a matter of healthy dispute. It claims to provide a multitude of services, as it sometimes even claims to be an end in itself. We are most inclined to see criticism as a constituent part of the same social process which produces the object of the criticism. It is especially appropriate to look at criticism in this way when the "object" itself has manifest social utility and intent, as is the case with public communication. The reciprocal action of the theory, practice, and criticism of speaking is significantly diminished when any one of these three aspects is neglected. Criticism nourishes both theory and practice. We have no particular illusion that the essays herein have had or will have a direct audience with the speakers who are analyzed, thus influencing the future efforts of these public figures, but we can foresee a rhetorical awareness and knowledgeability developing from the increased flow of critical materials. Assuming that the climate of critical sensitivity will be improved as such materials increase, we can look for perceptible improvement in the quality of the communication which influences and guides our society.

For those who may come cold to rhetorical criticism, we trust that we may be providing a dip into a literature which rests on a base of rich historical background and significant rhetorical theory, and which is now being renewed by the application of its techniques to contemporary communication.

An added usefulness of these studies is that they may provide a repository of data for future students of public address, that they may, in Wayne Brockriede's words of introduction to this series, provide "materials and insights which help the later, more thorough, scholarly critic."

The twenty-one essays which are included in this collection first appeared in the "Current Criticism" department of *Speaker and Gavel* between 1966 and 1970. No special effort was made to secure a coverage of particular types of speakers or critical approaches in this series. These studies were published because they were the best ones submitted during that period.

Still, taken as a whole, they have turned out to provide a colorful panorama of the significant themes and their spokesmen during this time. The agonies of the Vietnam decisions and the emergence of the "black power" issue strikingly dominate the concerns of speakers and critics alike, but other issues as well, ranging from the "death of God" to student protest, are given rhetorical analysis in these pages. Among black speakers who draw special attention here are Martin Luther King, Edward Brooke, Stokely Carmichael, and Malcolm X. Political figures appearing ubiquitously on the platform and the video screen demanded evaluation, so such individuals as Richard M. Nixon, Hubert Humphrey, Lyndon Johnson, and Spiro Agnew, as well as George Wallace (two essays), the Kennedys, Albert Gore, William Fulbright, and John Tower appear in these pages in major and minor roles.

Of some interest also is the suggestion of the wide range of methodologies which are available for dealing with the medium of public address, as illustrated in these essays, and the multitude of rhetorical tools used by these authors may indicate the kinds of choices which are open to the critic.

The nature and scope of this volume seem to us to be in resonance with some central concerns of the Speech Communication Association, especially as these concerns are manifested in the guidelines developed at the National Development Conference in Rhetoric sponsored by that association. It explores in a variety of ways the rhetoric of our times, defined broadly and treated comprehensively.

Delta Sigma Rho–Tau Kappa Alpha, national college honor society in forensics, has as its main purpose the recognition and encouragement of excellence in the arts of public communication. Through the publication of the quarterly *Speaker and Gavel*, as well as sponsorship of several annual award programs for individuals who have made substantial contributions to public life by means of their speaking, this organization has continually implemented its central purpose. Therefore, it is especially fitting for them to publish this collection of studies in current rhetorical criticism with the intent of contributing to the growing flow of such studies. We would like to give specific thanks to the members of the National Council of Delta Sigma Rho–Tau Kappa Alpha for their generous support of this collection. The "Current Criticism" feature was originated in *Speaker and Gavel* by Wayne E. Brockriede when he served as its editor. He presented a rationale for it (Vol. IV, No. 1), noting that criticism has a "special function" when completed soon after the discourse. Donald Torrence was associate editor in charge of Current Criticism for two years. We are also grateful for the encouragement and impetus provided by Robert L. Scott, who first suggested the idea of a collection of these studies. Finally, the authors who submitted their manuscripts to *Speaker and Gavel* and who have kindly permitted their reprinting here, deserve special thanks and appreciation.

Robert O. Weiss

Bernard L. Brock

CONTENTS

(Note: These articles are arranged in chronological order according
to their original appearance in *Speaker and Gavel*, extending from the November 1966 to the November 1970 issue.)

HUBERT HUMPHREY FACES THE "BLACK POWER" ISSUE

Robert L. Scott and Wayne Brockriede*

When Vice President Hubert H. Humphrey spoke to the 1,500 delegates of the NAACP convention in Los Angeles, July 6, 1966, he took a position on the major current issue confronting civil rights groups. Although the issue had not been drawn formally, it was nonetheless divisive. That issue was "Black Power."

At about the time Humphrey spoke, Stokely Carmichael said that he had heard the term used in one way and another since he was a child.[1] The phrase did not become a public symbolic issue, however, until it was introduced, presumably by Carmichael, during the Mississippi March which followed the shooting of James Meredith. By June 26, when the march climaxed in Jackson, Miss., "Black Power" was echoing throughout the country.[2]

By agreeing to speak at the NAACP convention, the Vice President appeared to signal the approval of the executive branch of the federal government with the stiffening opposition of Roy Wilkins and the NAACP and Martin Luther King and the SCLC toward Floyd McKissick and CORE and Stokely Carmichael and SNCC, opposition centering on the use of the Black Power phrase. Indeed, the day before the Humphrey speech, President Johnson told a news conference, "We are not interested in black power and we are not interested in white power. But we are interested in American democratic power, with a small 'd.'"[3]

In speaking to the delegates in Los Angeles and, through reports of the speech, to the nation, Humphrey had three choices: not to mention or allude to Black Power in any way, to treat it positively, or to treat it negatively. One might argue that the first choice was closed: his very being on the program constituted a position and, further, not to treat the issue would fail grievously to meet the expectations of his immediate and larger audiences. Perhaps the President's statements at his press conference closed the second choice to the Vice President. At any rate, Humphrey made the third choice.

---

* Mr. Scott is Professor of Speech at the University of Minnesota, and Mr. Brockriede is Professor of Speech at the University of Colorado.

[1] Associated Press release from Atlanta, Ga., of an interview with Stokely Carmichael, *Minneapolis Star*, July 7, 1966, p. 1. Carmichael used the Black Power phrase and the Black Panther slogan extensively during SNCC's voter registration drive in Lowndes County, Ala., during the past few years; see Andrew Kopkind, "The Lair of the Black Panther," *The New Republic*, Aug. 13, 1966, pp. 10–13. Another interesting use of the phrase prior to the Mississippi March is as the title of a series of articles dealing with Negro politicians during Southern Reconstruction days, 1867–1877; see Lerone Bennett, Jr., "Black Power," *Ebony*, Nov., 1965, pp. 28–38; Dec., 1965, pp. 51–60; Jan., 1966, pp. 116–22; Feb., 1966, pp. 127–38; April, 1966, pp. 121–31; and July, 1966, pp. 58–66.

[2] *Christian Science Monitor*, Midwest Edition, July 11, 1966, p. 1. A useful exposition of the development of the phrase, as well as a perceptive analysis of its issues, is Paul Good, "A White Look at Black Power," *Nation*, Aug. 8, 1966, pp. 112–17.

[3] *New York Times*, July 6, 1966, p. 18.

For the delegates at the NAACP convention and for those relatively few additional persons who read the complete speech as a message addressed to those delegates, the speech may well be judged a masterpiece of identification of the speaker and what he stands for with the audience and what it stands for.

The strategy of identification is apparent from the outset: "America is marching on the road to freedom. I am proud to be back among my friends of the NAACP who have led this march for 57 years."[4] These words identify both speaker and audience with a dominant symbol of the civil rights movement, the march. The speaker recalled the long history of NAACP involvement in the civil rights march, and many listeners must have known the speaker's own dedication to the cause. They may have remembered the 1948 Democratic convention when Humphrey risked his political future in the fight for a strong civil rights plank in the platform. Humphrey may have aided the recollection with his words, "For we have marched . . . even when our band was small and our ranks thin and ragged . . . even when victory seemed a distant and unattainable goal." Throughout the first section of the speech, the "march" motif dominates: "There have been young marchers and old . . . Negro and white . . . rich and poor . . . but always marching with a common spirit—moved by a common hope—and striving for a common objective." The motif suggests gradual progress, hard work, sacrifice, and cooperation; and it identifies the speaker with his NAACP audience.

The second section of the speech develops Humphrey's argument that neither he nor his listeners are, or should be, satisfied with past accomplishments. Civil rights workers and social scientists commonly express the belief that some of the restlessness and frustration in Negro ghettos stems from the male Negro's feeling that he is cut off from a positive, masculine role in his family and his community, cut off in some instances by a lack of education, cut off in others by a lack of opportunity to use what he has. Humphrey seemed to recognize this problem in a significant passage:

> A generation ago, it may have been enough for the Negro to ask for the right to enter a restaurant.
> But today the Negro American asks:
> Is my life better? Are my children attending better schools? Do I hold a better job—or any job? Do I have a voice in the life of my city and my neighborhood? Am I a first class citizen—a man among men, in my own eyes and in the eyes of my family?
> Until a man can truthfully answer "yes" to these questions, we should not expect him to consider the battle won or the struggle ended. And neither should we.

The long middle section of the speech is a catalog of past efforts by the federal government to alleviate conditions that irritate and frustrate, as well as a promise for more action in the future.

---

[4] U. S., *Congressional Record*, 89th Cong., 2nd Sess., July 12, 1966, Appendix, p. A3609. Mr. Humphrey's speech was inserted into the *Record* by Senator Warren G. Magnuson, Washington. All references to the Humphrey speech are to this printed version, pp. A3607–A3609.

The short third section fulfills several functions. Humphrey called for a realistic and cooperative struggle to achieve civil rights for all Americans. He encouraged those of like mind to persevere. The primary function, however, is to support the NAACP leadership on its position on the Black Power issue. One day before the Humphrey speech, Roy Wilkins had taken a vigorous stand on the issue in his keynote address to the delegates:

> No matter how endlessly they try to explain it, the term "black power" means antiwhite power. . . . It has to mean "going it alone." It has to mean separatism.
> Now, separatism, whether on the rarefied debate level of "black power" or on the wishful level of a Secessionist Freedom City in Watts, offers a disadvantaged minority little except a chance to shrivel and die. . . .
> We of the NAACP will have none of this. We have fought it too long. It is the ranging of race against race on the irrelevant basis of skin color.[5]

The Vice President endorsed Wilkins with a parallel statement on the issue:

> It seems to me fundamental that we cannot embrace the dogma of the oppressor—the notion that somehow a person's skin color determines his worthiness or unworthiness.
> Yes, racism is racism—and there is no room in America for racism of any color.
> And we must reject calls for racism, whether they come from a throat that is white or one that is black.
> We must strive to create a society in which the aims of the National Association for the Advancement of Colored People and the civil rights movement can be achieved. And, always remember, we seek *advancement* . . . not *apartheid*.

This passage placed Humphrey personally, and by implication the Johnson administration, behind the NAACP and SCLC in their struggle over the Black Power issue with SNCC and CORE. Humphrey had agreed with the majority of delegates who formed his immediate listening audience.[6] Three days after the speech, the convention ended after having passed a resolution described as virtually seeking "to establish the NAACP as the paramount organization that could decide which of the other groups are in the interest of Negroes and of the country, and which are not."[7]

---

[5] See *New York Times*, July 6, 1966, p. 14, for excerpts from Roy Wilkins' keynote address.

[6] Not all members of the NAACP oppose Black Power. One exception, for example, is the Rev. James Jones, a Negro member of the Los Angeles School Board. In a speech to the NAACP convention, after Wilkins' but before Humphrey's speech, Jones said: "An organization such as the NAACP should not be scared into a position of defense by the power structure with regard to the question of black power. [cheers] The NAACP must accept the challenge of defining black power and making it honorable and a factual part of the total power spectrum in America." Quoted in Nicholas von Hoffman, "Black Power Called Racism by Humphrey," *Washington Post*, July 7, 1966, p. A7.

[7] *Minneapolis Sunday Tribune*, July 10, 1966, p. 4A.

Viewed as an attempt to identify personally and substantively with the
NAACP delegates, Humphrey's speech was probably highly successful.
Humphrey had joined himself with the goals, values, and positions of the
NAACP and its leader, Roy Wilkins.

But the critic has a "second speech occasion" to evaluate when he considers Humphrey's address on July 6. The speaker is Hubert Humphrey as
he is revealed through the press and the broadcasting media. The audience
is the national audience, especially those persons and groups which have a
strong interest in the civil rights movement. The speech consists of excerpts which reporters conveyed to the national audience. With only a few
exceptions, press and broadcasting reports limited the "speech" to all or
parts of Humphrey's allusion to the Black Power issue in the passage quoted
above.[8]

The probable occurrence of the second occasion is predictable. Journalists would find newsworthy what a Vice President might say to a leading
civil rights organization about an explosive controversy. Also predictable
is the journalists' selection of the passage which relates to the Black Power
issue in strikingly figurative language.

Humphrey's "second" speech, addressed through the press to the national audience, may be judged a failure. The rhetorical circumstances,
in our judgment, made possible a great speech at a critical moment, but
Mr. Humphrey's analysis of the "second" occasion gave him at best a
mediocre speech.

The moment was critical because of the nature of Negro need and the
nature of the Black Power symbolic issue. Legislative gains had not been
transformed into substantial political or economic improvement for Negroes.
Discontent was deep, especially in riot-torn and riot-threatened ghettos,
and the feeling of powerlessness and frustration to effect significant change
led to a sense of desperation. The legislative approach shared by Wilkins
and King with the white liberals had become suspect.

Into this sense of need Stokely Carmichael and SNCC had introduced
the ambiguous phrase Black Power, and Floyd McKissick and CORE had
endorsed it in Baltimore.[9] The phrase implied *Black* Power, but left open
whether the leadership was to be exclusively Negro or whether cooperation
with white liberal forces was to be tolerated or sought. It further implied
Black *Power*, but left open the specific goals and methods. The phrase
threatened, but not clearly, not unequivocally. The black panther's message, "Move on over or we'll move on over you," may be seen as a counter-
part to the white rooster and "white supremacy." But the range of power-
seeking methods and the degree to which Black Power advocates might
move from nonviolence through violent self-defense to the initiation of
violent acts was yet to be determined.

Though ambiguous (and perhaps, in part, because ambiguous), the phrase
developed a fascinating appeal for many Negroes. It spoke to their condition in a way that "freedom now" and nonviolent "we shall overcome"

---

[8] Our treatment of Humphrey's address as "two speeches" raises an interesting
issue in the criticism of contemporary public address. To what extent does the
reporter function merely as a channel of communication and to what extent may
he be regarded as a more active rhetorical agent, as a part of the source com-
ponent in a communicative event?

[9] *U. S. News and World Report*, July 18, 1966, p. 31.

no longer did. Many Negroes agreed with Floyd McKissick's description of nonviolence as a "dying philosophy" that no longer can "be sold to the black people."[10] Black Power developed a kind of rhetorical magical power, and the events of the Mississippi March and the CORE convention revealed many Negroes ready to follow its banner. Where the banner would lead was still negotiable, and the very ambiguity of Black Power implied an attitude mobility inviting to rhetoricians.

How well did Hubert H. Humphrey meet this challenge in his address to the national audience? The first section of the speech to the NAACP delegates failed in its address to the national audience by default. The national audience never heard the "march" motif by means of which Humphrey had so adroitly identified with his physically present audience. Perhaps the journalists viewed this part of the discourse as too ordinary and too predictable to merit reporting.

The second section, again, failed by default. Again, journalists did not report to the national audience Mr. Humphrey's catalog of positive federal achievements, nor did they cite his promises for future action. Humphrey here claimed, "The next phase of the battle will be less dramatic, and it will attract a small number of those interested in the simple issues and the easy victories. Yet this next phase—one of the nuts and bolts of employment opportunities—is vital." But Mr. Humphrey did not specify the methods. He only made repeated abstractions of the sort quoted above. To those who are impatient, such promises seem excuses. In short, journalists perhaps properly regarded this portion of the speech as not worth reporting. The Vice President did little to advance the thinking on what gains should be expected through a continuation of the march toward freedom without an exercise of Black Power.

The third section, which journalists channeled to the national audience, failed by employing a negative divisive strategy. In a few well-turned sentences, Mr. Humphrey said "me, too," to Mr. Wilkins' prior rejection of Black Power, and placed the administration behind the NAACP. By implication, the essence of the Humphrey message was that Black Power adherents are racists, an accusation certain to alienate such people[11] and tending to force a decision from those who were wondering what attitude to adopt toward the ambiguous phrase, a decision as likely to go toward Black Power as away from it. Not only would a divisive strategy encourage a further splitting of the civil rights movement into two factions, but it would leave the militant faction in full possession of the symbol and in full control of determining its meaning.

"Yet we still think that there tends to be a panicky overreaction to the slogan 'black power,'" a *Christian Science Monitor* editorial said two days after Humphrey's speech.[12] Perhaps the editorial writer could have used the Vice President's speech as a basis for restructuring the response to the term had Humphrey chosen to have spoken differently.

Instead of a strategy of division, saying in effect, "There's the line, cross it at your peril," the Vice President's strategy could have been toward unification. Mr. Humphrey was in a unique position to help heal a breach

---

[10] Quoted in *ibid.*, p. 32.

[11] *New York Times*, July 8, 1966, p. 16, reports that CORE's Floyd McKissick was "visibly angry when asked to comment on remarks made by Mr. Humphrey."

[12] *Christian Science Monitor*, Midwest Edition, July 9, 1966, p. 14.

which two days after the speech Martin Luther King said threatened to split the civil rights movement permanently.[13] Furthermore, he had the opportunity to take the first step toward de-fusing the explosive Black Power phrase.

Did the Vice President really have a good opportunity to unify the movement and to de-fuse the phrase? "No matter how endlessly they try to explain it, the term 'black power' means antiwhite power," Wilkins had said in his keynote address. But that "they" are "endlessly" explaining it indicates that the meaning of the concept is in the process of being worked out. "It is necessary for Negroes to have power," Martin Luther King said in Chicago the day Humphrey spoke in Los Angeles, "We've got to have political power. I don't use the phrase 'black power' because it gives the wrong impression. . . . We do not want to substitute one tyranny for another."[14] Could Mr. Humphrey have helped make Black Power mean political and economic power for Negroes? Certainly the administration stands for increasing Negroes' political and economic power in certain specified ways. Could he have suggested ways in which Negroes might participate more vigorously in achieving certain other specified goals so that power could be used *by* the blacks as well as *for* them?[15] Could he have encouraged civil rights leaders to use the term in less menacing ways?

The person most closely identified with the phrase, Stokely Carmichael, has indicated that the term is open to a pacific interpretation. In his interview with the press the day after Humphrey spoke, he responded to the question, "Roy Wilkins . . . has said no matter how you say it, it means antiwhite. What's your view?" by replying, "Well, I've never used that word and I don't see why the rallying cry of black power would mean that."[16] Mr. Carmichael compared the impulse behind Black Power with the banding together of workers in labor unions to make their demands felt. Here is an analogy that a man like Hubert Humphrey should have been able to see and to exploit.[17]

For the Vice President to have identified himself with a pacific interpretation of Black Power would have recognized the need of Negroes for power exercised in their behalf and also their need to do some of the exercising. It could have aided tendencies toward cooperation and unification of civil rights groups. The strategy is perhaps not an obvious one, nor is it one easily made effective. Given the rhetorical climate in which Mr. Humphrey worked, however, such a choice could have made possible a truly great speech. The choice he made allowed him to identify skillfully with the NAACP and Roy Wilkins. Even assuming the wisdom of rejecting Black Power, however, such a choice allowed the Vice President only to echo Roy Wilkins' keynote address. Given his office and his ability, this much is too little to expect from Hubert Humphrey.

[13] *New York Times*, July 9, 1966, p. 1.

[14] *Minneapolis Star*, July 7, 1966, p. 2A.

[15] Martin Luther King recognized this aspect of Black Power: "[If it is] . . . an appeal to racial pride, an appeal to the Negro not to be ashamed of being black, and the transfer of the powerlessness of the Negro into positive, constructive power . . . then I agree with it" (quoted in *Christian Science Monitor*, July 11, 1966, p. 3).

[16] *Minneapolis Star*, July 7, 1966, p. 1A.

[17] James Jones also suggests the value of defining Black Power (see fn. 7). Had the statement of Jones been made by someone as visible as Humphrey, it might have packed a greater rhetorical wallop.

BROOKE'S DILEMMA

Harry P. Kerr*

Edward W. Brooke has on him the mark of greatness.

Massachusetts' new junior Senator is the most promising political figure to emerge from the Bay State in recent years—more promising at this point in their respective careers than John F. Kennedy. The steps he chooses to take in attempting to traverse the road to national prominence will almost certainly constitute one of the fascinating political stories of the sixties. And this would be true even if Brooke were not a Negro.

Brooke's style in state politics is probably a reliable indicator of the image he will try to develop in Washington. Whether or not his success in Massachusetts can be duplicated on a national scale is much less certain.

Some believe that Brooke gained support because he is a Negro, that Brooke votes have been conscience votes (and cheap penance at that since Brooke repudiates militant Negro organizations). Perhaps so, but I can find little direct or indirect confirmation in talking with voters. White voters who are asked what effect Brooke's color has on their feelings toward him most often respond: "I don't think of Brooke as a Negro."

The public statement may not be seriously at odds with the truth. Brooke's reputation for honesty and effectiveness has largely submerged the fact of his race. In eighteen months as chairman of Boston's watchdog Finance Commission and four subsequent years as Attorney General of the Commonwealth, he prosecuted venal politicians, made graft more dangerous by revising procedures for handling state funds, exposed contractors who substituted covert payments for cement, and all the while remained untouched by any hint of dishonesty or political maneuvering.

An electorate which has learned the expensive way to regard politicians with suspicion and which cannot be dissuaded that too many hands are in the statehouse till responded to Brooke's atypical record with overwhelming support. His term as Finance Commission chairman earned 1,143,065 votes and a plurality of 259,355 in his first campaign for the office of Attorney General in 1962. The incumbent Republican governor, John A. Volpe, was defeated by Endicott Peabody that year and no other Republican was elected to state-wide office.

In 1964 Volpe defeated Peabody handily, but Brooke led the ticket with 1,543,900 votes and a plurality of 797,510, the largest achieved by any Republican in the history of Massachusetts. Brooke carried every city in the state and all but two of its towns.

Volpe has been reelected governor again this year with a total vote estimated at slightly over 1,250,000 and a plurality of about 550,000. Brooke's margin over Peabody in the senatorial race was smaller but still substantial: a plurality of about 430,000 and a total vote just over 1,200,000. (The extent to which Massachusetts avoided a "white backlash," incidentally, is indicated by the fact that fewer than 5,000 of the two million people who cast votes for a gubernatorial candidate failed to vote in a senate race which pitted a Negro against a very liberal white.)

Since Peabody's reputation for honesty equals Brooke's, one must look to other differentiating factors. The most obvious is statesmanship, Brooke's

---

* Mr. Kerr is Associate Professor of Speech at Harvard University.

other long suit and the one quality Peabody lacks conspicuously.

Brooke's Attorney General was not a two-fisted racket buster. He was thoughtful, methodical, inexorable. In typical photographs Brooke studies a law book or ponders a decision with head on hand. He recruited talented young lawyers as Assistant Attorneys General, and took as much credit for their recruitment as for the actions their work made possible. His office proposed an average of forty pieces of legislation a year (including a high-way codification bill which ran to 390 pages), significantly reduced the backlog of land damage cases, received and processed through a new agency some three thousand complaints of wrongdoing, and successfully sought indictments of more than a hundred individuals and corporations for alleged larceny, conspiracy, and bribery.

The image which Brooke projects in public appearances complements the no-nonsense atmosphere of his office. On the few occasions when he has allowed strong feelings to color his speech—as in the striking remarks following Peabody's concession in the early hours of November 9th—Brooke has demonstrated that he can inspire and incite. His voice is deep, flexible, and pleasing, his face expressive, his gestures easy, and his instincts those of the accomplished platform orator.

But he much prefers measured tones and measured language. Pyrotechnics have been less in evidence than the intelligence, humanity, and determina-tion he displays most convincingly in conversational style. His delivery is typically low-keyed, deliberate. The language is clear and efficient, figured sparingly, and as free from striking phrases as it is from clichés. The sub-stance is solid: he speaks to difficult questions more directly than most, eschews platitudes, and takes the shorter course when two words will do as well as three.

He extemporizes easily and effectively with or without notes and handles a manuscript well. Listeners do not lose their awareness of his presence. When Brooke speaks, the speech *is* Brooke; his personality is strong, attrac-tive, admirable. He wins supporters without seeming to plead his case.

The dominant tone is competence and in Massachusetts it was enough. Competence set him off sharply from the likeable but bumbling Peabody and induced a million two hundred thousand Bay Staters to vote for a statesman who happened to be a Negro. But will competence plus a degree of subdued personal magnetism be enough to impress a broader electorate or, indeed, enough to defeat a future opponent who sparks voter imagination? The history of electronic campaigning suggests that Brooke cannot increase his national stature—and perhaps not even maintain it—without the pyro-technics he now avoids.

Therein lies Brooke's dilemma. Full utilization of his undoubted capacity for stirring, articulate speech is probably essential, but it also would probably be fatal. Brooke's political success has required dissociation from the Negro stereotype. Although they have elected the first Negro Senator of this century, Massachusetts voters did not cast their ballots for a Negro. They voted for integrity and competence of a high order—qualities not present in the Negro stereotype. Eloquence unfortunately is. Brooke delivering a spirited address to a political rally would look and sound to too many white voters too much like Stokely Carmichael inciting a riot.

Whether the nation will focus on Brooke's qualities rather than his color is the central issue which makes his career in Washington especially inter-esting and important.

THE POWELL AFFAIR

PETER E. KANE*

One of the more interesting legislative debates in recent years took place on the floor of the United States House of Representatives on the afternoon of March 1, 1967. The question debated that afternoon was that of the seating of Representative Adam Clayton Powell, eleven-term Negro Congressman from Harlem. The following will examine the context in which the debate took place and then the debate itself.

One of the most important but unspoken problems to face the Ninetieth Congress is the marked decline of public confidence in the legislative branch of the Federal government. Public opinion surveys clearly show increasing doubts about the competence and integrity of Congress. The origins of these doubts are twofold. First, the archaic procedures used by Congress are not adequate to meet the demands placed upon a national legislature in the mid-twentieth century. Second, the abuse of personal power by individuals and groups of Congressmen has tarnished the reputation of the entire legislature.[1] On the Senate side of the hill the problem has been confronted in the extended debate on legislative reorganization. On the House side the problem was personified in Adam Clayton Powell.

Representative Powell was first elected to Congress by his Harlem constituency in 1944. Over the years he served without any particular distinction until the inexorable passage of time and the rules of seniority brought him to the chair of the House Education and Labor Committee. Under his chairmanship this committee brought to the floor of the House many of the major pieces of legislation upon which President Johnson's "Great Society" is based.

Like many other Congressmen, Representative Powell used his position to further his own as well as the public's welfare. Traditionally Congress has ignored the fairly common practices of "investigation" trips to popular resorts and relatives on Congressional payrolls. Such practices were in effect viewed as normal perquisites of the office. In addition any moral wrongdoing was either just ignored or actually covered up as Congressmen protected fellow members of the club. This latter posture is probably no better illustrated than in the House reaction last year to published comments about Representative L. Mendel Rivers' drinking problem. Rivers' appearance on the House floor following this disclosure was greeted with a standing ovation.[2]

The essential difference between the Powell case and that of other Congressmen is one of publicity. Other representatives convicted on more serious charges have continued their Congressional careers with little notice.[3] Unlike his colleagues, Powell was never particularly circumspect about his activities. The hiring of beauty queen Corinne Huff as an Administrative Assistant for his committee staff and the many trips he

---

* Mr. Kane is Director of Forensics and Instructor of Speech at Harpur College.
[1] Theodore Sorensen, "Reforming Congress," *Saturday Review*, XLIX (July 16, 1966), 22.
[2] "Vote for Non-Leadership," *Time*, LXXVII (June 24, 1966), 24.
[3] "No Home in the House," *Time*, LXXXIX (March 10, 1967), 20.

took with her were widely publicized. His real problems began, however, with his loss of a libel suit to one of his Harlem constituents. In a
major strategic error Powell refused to pay the judgment against him.
Continued adjudication of this dispute not only increased the judgment
fourfold and resulted in contempt citations, but also attracted even greater
public attention to himself and his activities.[4] Powell's legal problems
eventually reached the point where he was unable to enter his home
state because of outstanding warrants for his arrest.

The Powell situation was complicated by his race. Although he is only
in small part of Negro origin and could probably "pass" as white, Powell
has identified himself as a Negro and is identified in the public mind
as a Negro. His position in Congress made him the most politically powerful
Negro in the country. As such he became the symbol of success and
"Black Power" for many.

Following his 1966 re-election in which he won 74% of the vote cast
without ever appearing in his Congressional district, a subcommittee of
the House Administration Committee began an investigation of Powell's
activities. The hearings under committee chairman Wayne L. Hays, Ohio
Democrat, revealed questionable expenditures of travel funds and that
Powell's wife, listed by her maiden name as Administrative Assistant on
his Congressional staff, had been living in Puerto Rico, had done no work,
and had not received her pay checks although someone had signed and
cashed them.[5]

One of the fundamental issues involved in the Powell case arose during
this hearing. In response to a request to cooperate, Representative Powell
stated that he would do so providing the committee expand its investigation to include other representatives and House committees. In rejecting
these conditions for cooperation, the subcommittee lent weight to the
charge that the House was out to get Powell rather than eliminate questionable practices.[6]

The formal recognition of Representative Powell's activities led to demands that the House take action against him. On January 3 the House
Administration Committee issued a twelve-point report of their findings.[7]
On the basis of these findings Representative Lionell Van Deerlin, California Democrat, stated that he would challenge Powell's right to be sworn
when the Ninetieth Congress convened.[8] The House Democratic Party
leadership suggested alternative punishment. The party caucus might
strip Powell of his seniority rights and chairmanship as it had Representatives John Bell Williams of Mississippi and Albert W. Watson of South
Carolina who had supported Barry Goldwater in the 1964 presidential
election.[9] In response Powell issued a statement in which he charged that
his critics were "motivated by the desire to politically castrate one of

---

[4] *The New York Times* for 1965 ran more than sixty separate articles on
Powell's legal problems.

[5] "Adam & Yvette," *Time*, LXXXIX (Feb. 24, 1967), 18.

[6] "Powell Actions," *Congressional Quarterly Weekly Report*, XXIV (Dec. 23,
1966), 3068.

[7] *The New York Times*, January 4, 1967, p. 1.

[8] "Unseating Powell," *Congressional Quarterly Weekly Report*, XXIV (Jan.
13, 1967), 26.

[9] *Ibid.*, 25.

America's most powerful Negroes."[10] With this charge Representative Powell made explicit the racial dimension of the case.

The Democratic caucus on January 9 voted to replace Representative Powell as chairman of the House Education and Labor Committee but took no action on his seniority.[11] The hope that this step would head off any further disciplinary action was not realized. The following day Powell was asked to stand aside while the rest of the House took the oath of office. Representative Van Deerlin was prevented from moving that Powell be barred by the motion introduced by Representative Morris K. Udall, Arizona Democrat, which would postpone the seating of Representative Powell for 60 days so that a select committee could investigate and make recommendations to the House. The Udall motion was passed by a 363 to 65 roll call vote. The 65 representatives opposing the resolution and supporting the seating of Powell were all Democrats.[12]

On February 8 Representative Powell appeared before the nine-member committee selected by House Speaker John W. McCormack, Massachusetts Democrat. Powell's lawyers introduced a series of motions challenging the right of the committee to examine their client. The most important of these six motions maintained that the committee had the right to consider only the constitutional requirements of age, citizenship, and inhabitancy. Powell refused to say anything to the committee other than that he was born in New Haven, Connecticut, in 1908, had moved to New York City when he was six months old, and lived at 120 West 138th Street. Although the select committee rejected his six motions, Powell had again succeeded in raising a fundamental issue. Since Article I, Section 2, of the Constitution lists only age, citizenship, and residence as requirements for holding the office of Representative, Powell maintained that he could be barred only on one of these grounds. He interpreted Article I, Section 5, "Each House shall be the judge of the elections, returns and qualifications of its own members," to mean that the legitimacy of his election could be examined, but this point had not been challenged.[13] In the area of the legal powers of the House there were no clear precedents. In 1900 the House excluded Representative-Elect Brigham H. Roberts, Utah Democrat, because he was an admitted polygamist.[14] In 1933 it seated Representative-Elect Francis H. Shoemaker, Minnesota Farmer-Laborite, even though he had been convicted and sentenced to prison.[15] The other cases of House action also failed to provide a clear precedent.

In its report of February 23 the Select Committee noted that Representative Powell had fulfilled the constitutional qualifications for office but was guilty of improper conduct. The committee recommended that Powell be seated and formally censured. Further, he should pay $40,000 as partial restitution of misappropriated funds, and all prior seniority rights should

[10] "Powell's Statement," *Congressional Quarterly Weekly Report*, XXV (Jan. 13, 1967), 50.

[11] "Powell Loses Chairmanship; Seat in Doubt," *Congressional Quarterly Weekly Report*, XXV (Jan. 13, 1967), 47.

[12] *Ibid.*

[13] "Powell Strategy Raises Constitutional Questions," *Congressional Quarterly Weekly Report*, XXV (Feb. 17, 1967), 247–48.

[14] *Ibid.*, 248.

[15] *Ibid.*

be removed. Finally, the committee recommended investigations of the activities of other representatives and House committees.[16] This report which was the subject of the March 1 debate managed to deal with three of the four issues in the Powell case. Powell would be severely punished for his public wrongdoing. Since he would be seated, the constitutional question would not be resolved. The call for other investigations answered the charge that Powell had been singled out for punishment. This call in part answered the racial charge which could in fact only be fully denied if the House took no punitive action. These last two points were underlined by Representative John Conyers, Jr., Michigan Democrat, the Negro member of the Select Committee, who stated that he would discount personal and racial bias if the House did in fact investigate and punish other members.[17]

The context of the debate on the floor of the House, therefore, was whether to accept the report of the Select Committee. In opening the two-hour debate, Committee Chairman Emanuel Celler, New York Democrat, made three points. First, he asked "that we set all passions aside" and reach a decision on a strictly legal and rational basis.[18] Second, the punishment called for in the report was severe.

> Censure is a dreadful act to contemplate. Imagine, if you will, yourself walking down the aisle of this Chamber accompanied by the Sergeant at Arms, and in the well of the House listening to the strictures placed upon you by the Speaker in the presence of your colleagues.[19]

Third, Representative Celler noted not only that exclusion or expulsion would be an easy punishment in comparison to censure, but also that such action would lead the House into highly questionable constitutional considerations. He noted that both Madison and Hamilton in the Federalist papers had stated that the House did not have the right to set qualifications for its own membership.[20]

The ranking Republican member of the Select Committee, Representative Arch A. Moore, Jr., of West Virginia, spoke in support of all three of these points and added a fourth. In opposition to exclusion he pointed out, "If we turn him out, his constituency will turn him back with an even greater majority."[21] This well-taken point was one which failed to receive the consideration it deserved. At the end of the debate the question of what the House would do if Adam Clayton Powell were re-elected had not been answered.

Only one real attempt to deal with the problem posed by Representative Moore was made. Representative Clarence D. Long, Maryland Democrat, speaking against seating Representative Powell, said, "Any responsibility for returning Mr. Powell to his seat should rest on his constituents and the House should not assume in advance that they will not live up to that responsibility."[22] While this solution was logically valid, it ignored the political realities of the situation. No objective political

---

[16] *The New York Times*, Feb. 24, 1967, p. 1.
[17] *Ibid.*
[18] U. S., *Congressional Record*, 90th Cong., 1st Sess., 1967, H1919.
[19] *Ibid.*, H1920.
[20] *Ibid.*
[21] *Ibid.*, H1921.
[22] *Ibid.*, H1922.

observer could claim that Harlem would not re-elect Powell if he were a candidate.

Representative Long went on to examine the constitutional arguments which had been advanced in favor of accepting the committee report. He pointed out that no court had ever considered previous exclusions.

> Two strong doctrines, in fact, militate against such court consideration.
> First is the doctrine of separation of powers; the Constitution provides that each House shall be the judge of the elections, returns, and qualifications of its Members.
> Second is the political questions doctrine. The courts will not handle questions inherently in the power of other coordinate branches at the same level of Government.[23]

Except for reiterating that Powell met the constitutional requirements of age, citizenship, and residency, Representative Long's argument went unchallenged. As he himself had pointed out, no precedents provided guidance in this area. However, the supporters of the committee report might have called attention to the whole principle of judicial review. Review and often reversal of contempt of Congress citations suggests that the courts can review not only legislation but other actions of Congress as well.

The emotionalism which Representative Celler sought to avoid was nowhere more clearly demonstrated than in the speech of Representative Watson, who had become a Republican since the removal of his seniority by the Democratic caucus in 1965.

> Ladies and gentlemen, we are not deciding the fate of one Adam Clayton Powell. Indeed, we are deciding the fate of this House of Representatives.
>
> . . . .
>
> The public knows that Powell is guilty; the public knows that he is a fugitive from justice. The public knows that he has flaunted and flouted the courts of the great State of New York. The public knows that he is charged with defrauding the taxpayers of the United States of America. The public knows that he had the responsibility as a Member of this body to conduct himself in such manner as to reflect credit both upon this body and the people of this country. The public knows that he is not on trial; but, no, you and I are on trial. . . .
>
> . . . .
>
> Mr. Speaker, much has been said here about "annihilation by humiliation." We cannot believe Powell can be humiliated. Is there a humiliating bone in the body of the man under discussion? Has he displayed any repentance or given any indication that he is regretful? Why, even at this moment, Mr. Speaker, as we are debating this agonizing and difficult issue, where is Adam Clayton Powell? As far as I know he is down in Bimini with a glass in one hand and a woman in the other. Can you think a man so calloused to his fate today can be humiliated? Certainly none could logically contend that.[24]

In this highly emotive manner Representative Watson made one of the few explicit references in the entire debate to the underlying question in the Powell case: declining public confidence in Congress.

In keeping with Representative Celler's original request, none of the

---

[23] *Ibid.*
[24] *Ibid.*, H1923.

supporters of the committee report responded emotionally to the remarks of Representative Watson. One committee member, Republican Charles M. Teague of California, commented obliquely as follows:

> Mr. Speaker, several Members on both sides of the aisle have told me within the last few days that they are satisfied that the recommendations of the select committee are sound and should be adopted but they were afraid that they could not vote to do so. They said that their mail was 100 to 1 to "throw the rascal out" and that under this kind of pressure, it would be most difficult for them to vote to seat Adam Clayton Powell even with the severe punishment we have suggested.
>
> . . . .
>
> I am sure that we have all read John F. Kennedy's book "Profiles in Courage." Perhaps some small amount of courage might be required to vote to seat, censure, and punish Mr. Powell, but I suggest not much.[25]

The most significant element in Representative Teague's remark is that it, like Representative Watson's statement, underlines the factor of the publicity which Powell's wrongdoing received. Both the well-reported hearings and Representative Powell's own lack of discretion had created public awareness and interest which manifested itself in forceful public demand for corrective action.

The longest speech of the debate was made by Representative Conyers, the Negro member of the Select Committee. In this speech Conyers reviewed again the constitutional arguments for seating Powell and went on to examine in detail prior cases of House censure for financial misconduct. These cases showed that in situations similar to the Powell case the House had found censure alone to be a suitable punishment. Conyers, in fact, objected to the proposed punishment beyond censure and suggested that the punishment and the public pressure for it were at least in part racially motivated. He concluded by calling attention to the special role which Powell plays in the American scene.

> But there is something else about Adam Powell, the symbol of Negro America, a personal hero of mine, that makes this a tragedy that I cannot do other than make sure every Member on this floor is perfectly cognizant of before we, hopefully, vote for the previous question here today.
>
> The Congressman Adam Clayton Powell is a false caricature of the Powell, to whom the churches, the synagogues, the labor unions and educational institutions—not just black Americans but all Americans—owe an unparalleled debt for the unexcelled legislation that has been in the House of Representatives under his leadership as the chairman of the Committee on Education and Labor.
>
> It is Adam Clayton Powell who has steered through the Manpower Development Training Act, the antipoverty bill, the Juvenile Delinquency Act, the Vocational Education Act, the National Defense Education Act and all of these bills which have redounded to the benefit not only of Negro Americans but to the benefit of all Americans.[26]

A short time after Representative Conyers finished speaking the two hours allotted for debate expired. Representative Celler's motion to end debate and vote on the committee report was defeated 202 to 222.[27]

---

[25] *Ibid.*, 1924.
[26] *Ibid.*, 1929.
[27] *Ibid.*, 1941–42.

Representative Thomas B. Curtis, Missouri Republican, then offered an amendment as a substitute for the committee report. The amendment flatly excluded Representative Powell from the Ninetieth Congress.[28] Two arguments were presented by Representative Curtis and others in support of this amendment. The first, the "throw the rascal out" argument, consisted of a review of the wrongdoings of Adam Clayton Powell. The second dealt with the legality of exclusion. Neither argument was developed beyond what had already been stated. Representative Curtis moved the previous question which was carried by a 263 to 161 vote. The amendment was agreed to by a vote of 248 to 176, and the amended report passed 307 to 116. On the key vote to accept the amendment the Democrats were about evenly split while the Republicans voted better than two to one in support of the amendment. The formal leadership of both parties voted with the minority.[29]

As is often the case in legislative debating, the consideration and disposition of the case of Adam Clayton Powell in the House of Representatives settled little. While his lawyers are pursuing the matter in the courts, Powell with great ease won re-election in the special election to fill his vacant seat. Until such time as the courts act it will not be known if the House can exclude a member on grounds other than age, citizenship, residency, or validity of election. Reaction to the Powell exclusion demonstrates that a great many people consider the action racially motivated. While race did play a part, there is no way to know exactly how important a part. One answer to this question will be found in degree of diligence exercised by the House in exposing and punishing other wrongdoers. Already the Powell case has resulted in the introduction of almost one hundred different proposals for establishing a code of ethics, a permanent investigating committee, and/or standard procedures for punishing wayward representatives.[30] If something were to come of these proposals, a major step might be taken toward the restoration of public confidence in the Congress.

---

[28] *Ibid.*, 1942.
[29] *Ibid.*, H1955–57.
[30] *The New York Times*, March 17, 1967, p. 13.

INSULARITY, RHETORIC, AND GENERAL CHARLES DE GAULLE

Mary Reeves*

Any inquiry into the rhetoric of General Charles de Gaulle must begin with de Gaulle the man. The only major politician on the contemporary scene who survived World War II, de Gaulle has become one of the most controversial men of all times. Flora Lewis, syndicated foreign affairs columnist, writes in the *New York Times Magazine* that one in doubt as to the complexity of this man need only ask the people whom he governs: "What does Gaullism mean?" Their answers range from "a sentiment for France" to "a noise, a headstrong arrogance" to "nothing."[1] Amid the diversity of answers there is, however, a strain of consistency. Gaullism, defined by negation, is not a political system or philosophy. Reactions to the term are reactions to the person, de Gaulle, rather than to a specific ideology.

Alexander Werth, political biographer of de Gaulle, feels that the opening passage of de Gaulle's *Memoires* gives, perhaps, the clearest explication of his deep feeling for his country.

> I early came to believe that France, like the Princess in a fairy tale or the Madonna of the Frescoes, had an eminent and exceptional destiny. . . . Our country must, under pain of mortal danger, aim high and stand upright. In short, France as I see her, cannot be France without greatness.[2]

Coupled with this vision of France's destiny is General de Gaulle's conviction that no man can serve France as well as he. In short, he is France and France is destined to greatness. The acceptance of this philosophy was exemplified when a German Common-Market official was asked "whether it was not absurd that one *country* could impose its will on five others?" The official replied, "Great *men* are like that."[3]

The focus of this paper will be General de Gaulle's recent (May 16, 1967) speech dealing with Great Britain's application for membership in the European Economic Community.[4] Material dealing with the "no entry" of Great Britain dominated the last twenty minutes of General de Gaulle's eighty-minute press conference held in the Salle des Fetes of the Elysee Palace. The May 16th speech needs to be examined in relation to two preceding speeches. One was given by General de Gaulle January 14, 1963 after eighteen months of negotiating concerning Britain's membership in the European Economic Community.[5] The other was given by Harold Wilson May 8, 1967 preceding the 488–62 vote in the House of Commons favoring Britain's application for membership in the Common Market.[6]

---

* The author is an instructor in speech at Northeast Missouri State Teachers College.

[1] May 14, 1967, p. 26.

[2] Alexander Werth, *De Gaulle* (New York: Simon and Schuster, 1966), p. 57.

[3] *The London Times*, May 20, 1967, p. 3.

[4] *Vital Speeches of the Day*, June 1, 1967, pp. 495–97. All references to de Gaulle's May 16, 1967 speech are to this printed version.

[5] *Vital Speeches of the Day*, Feb. 1, 1963, pp. 232–33. All references to de Gaulle's Jan. 14, 1963 speech are to this printed version.

[6] *Vital Speeches of the Day*, June 1, 1967, pp. 482–94. All references to Harold Wilson's May 8, 1967 speech are to this printed version.

De Gaulle's 1963 comments regarding Great Britain were also part of a longer news conference. The remarks were not, however, impromptu in nature. De Gaulle prepares such television performances meticulously. Alexander Werth describes this process in detail in his biography of de Gaulle when he states that de Gaulle writes out his text, memorizes it, practices in front of a mirror, and has even gone to the trouble to take lessons in diction from an actor in the Comedie Francaise. He invites questions from the reporters ahead of time, then contorts them so as to label the broad areas that he has previously decided he wants to cover. In no way could either of these speeches be considered to be less than carefully calculated pronouncements on Britain's advances to the European Economic Community.

Technically, the 1963 speech was not a veto of Britain's efforts because Great Britain had not officially applied for membership. The speech was, however, worded in such a fashion that negotiations stopped and Great Britain did not submit a bid for entry. At that time, according to C. L. Sulzberger writing in the *New York Times*, de Gaulle prophesied that Mac-Millan's defeat would doom the tories; the subsequent labor government would "make such a mess of things that when the conservatives came back they would seek membership on any terms."[7]

General de Gaulle may have been somewhat surprised to find labor-leader Harold Wilson speaking for Britain's application only four years later. The Wilson speech was a carefully prepared and lengthy explanation of the conditions governing Britain's current application to the EEC. It represented a capsule reappraisal of the dynamic changes in the interim between the two de Gaulle pronouncements.

De Gaulle's May 16, 1967 speech did not function immediately as a veto. If the purpose were to quell British action, it failed. If the purpose were to subdue British optimism, it succeeded.

Anthony Lewis writing from London for the *New York Times* carefully considers and refutes de Gaulle's basic arguments against entry. In conclusion, he mentions that de Gaulle in a passing phrase referred to Britain as an island. Mr. Lewis suggests that de Gaulle's economical and political theories are open to reproach, but that his geography is impeccable.[8] No doubt General de Gaulle was referring to Great Britain's insularity in more than merely geographical terms. Just such an interpretation defines the chief characteristic of General Charles de Gaulle's rhetoric of May 16th. It is, indeed, isolated: isolated from the changes that have occurred in the last four years, isolated from the arguments advanced by the government of Harold Wilson, and even isolated in the scope of its intended audience.

Before turning to an analysis of the content of the speech, an examination of the scope of the audience seems requisite as a means of demonstrating insularity. May 16, 1967 provided a background of political agitation for de Gaulle's speech. At de Gaulle's instigation, Premier Pompidou had presented the legislature with a request for the power to govern by decree in social and economic affairs for six months. According to the *New York Times* of May 17th, the major labor unions had called a nationwide strike in protest against this request. Given the dimensions of this strike activity, one can necessarily conclude that General de Gaulle knew that his press conference would not have wide mass media coverage in France.

---

[7] May 17, 1967, p. 46.
[8] May 18, 1967, p. 18.

Printers and journalists started a walkout at 5 this afternoon (Tuesday afternoon of the speech). As a result there will be no morning newspapers tomorrow and the text of the President's news conference will not be printed until Thursday.[9]

Two afternoon papers in Paris were able to carry an incomplete report of the press conference; but since de Gaulle had held the remarks concerning Britain and the EEC until the end of the conference, this material was not included in the sketchy reports. Thus, the strike prevented readers from receiving news of the press conference; furthermore, the extreme chaos caused by a nationwide general strike tended to divert the attention of Frenchmen away from a consideration of Great Britain and the Common Market when they did receive the news. According to *The London Times*, May 18, 1967:

Reaction to General de Gaulle's press conference yesterday, and particularly to his detailed treatment of Britain's entry into Europe, were muted today because of the general strike which deprived France of newspapers.[10]

De Gaulle had to know that this reaction would occur. Maybe an inkling of the reason for the strategic positioning of the EEC pronouncement can be found in this quotation reported by Richard E. Mooney in the *New York Times* of May 21, 1967. Mooney is quoting from *Le Monde*, widely regarded as France's most respected daily.

The only way to settle this issue is to negotiate without delay. We are pleased that our partner countries have decided to proceed this way and not to become discouraged too quickly just because the general has raised his voice.[11]

Thus, one may perceive a definite aura of "isolatedness" surrounding de Gaulle's chosen audience. The British and American newspaper headlines must have pleased the General. For example, from London came "General de Gaulle Says It Again,"[12] and the *New York Times* cited a West European diplomat's comment: "It was a 20-minute burial of Britain's chances."[13] The follow-up reports were, however, more reflective and exemplified the determination that has characterized Great Britain's recent drive for admission: "Not Taking Non for an Answer."[14]

The content of de Gaulle's recent speech provides the most obvious aspects of insularity. The major arguments advanced by General de Gaulle January 14, 1963 were:

1. The Treaty of Rome was concluded among six continental countries that are adjacent, an outside country with less political and military solidarity would be a disruptive force in such an arrangement (insularity argument).
2. The British agricultural system, largely based on importing foodstuffs purchased at low prices, would be incompatible with the policy of the EEC as it stands (agricultural argument).
3. Great Britain is linked to certain other countries by "special" political or military agreements. The United States would inch her way in and form an Atlantic Community that "would soon completely swallow up the European Community" (Trojan Horse argument).

---

[9] *New York Times*, May 17, 1967, p. 14.
[10] P. 5.
[11] P. 10.
[12] The *London Times*, May 17, 1967, p. 1.
[13] May 17, 1967, p. 1.
[14] *The London Times*, May 17, 1967, p. 9.

    4. Great Britain's own evolution and the evolution of the world *might* at some time create such conditions that membership would be possible (remote possibility argument).

Harold Wilson's May 8th speech gives a primary emphasis to the concept of dynamism. It sets forth in no uncertain terms that Great Britain's position has changed. Admittedly, the strong antimarket attitude of the Labor Party of four years ago is a little difficult to forget, and the virtually unattainable "essential conditions" to be met before Britain would consider entry are, no doubt, residual in the minds of many. Times have, however, changed.

As far as the new attitudes toward the Common Market, the Wilson speech speaks for itself:

    1. "So far as British industry is concerned, we seek no exemption from the obligations which fall upon every member of the Community."

    2. "We have to decide whether or not to apply for entry to a Community which is characterized by this particular agricultural system. It is useless to think we can wish it away and I should be misleading the House if I said that this policy is negotiable. We have to come to terms with it."

    3. Concerning political issues: "Her Majesty's Government are prepared to accept the same obligations as our prospective Common Market colleagues—no more, no less."

Couple these official pronouncements with such editorial comments as the following by C. L. Sulzberger writing from Paris for the *New York Times*:

> Once-imperial Britian has been spending the past few months doing everything Harold Wilson can imagine to prove that England is part of Europe—that is, everything except filling in the channel. It even wants to tunnel under the channel to France,[15]

and headlines from recent United States news magazines: "Is U. S. Losing Britain Its No. 1 Ally?"[16] and you have a more realistic picture of the status quo.

Having examined the background of content in the two previous speeches, we turn to de Gaulle's recent speech. The speech begins with a foreboding air when de Gaulle states he doesn't want "to prejudge what the negotiations, if they take place—I repeat, if they take place—would be about." Depending on how you read this phrase, you may say that de Gaulle doubts that negotiations will occur or he is admitting the inevitability of their occurrence. At least he is not categorically saying they won't occur. Prejudgment, in spite of the verbal disavowal of its use, characterizes the speech. The opening of the speech outlines three alternatives that must be contemplated by anyone wishing to change the status quo.

    1. The first is to admit Great Britain with all the exemptions and new conditions such an entry would entail. The consequence of such action would be "destructive upheavals" and a prelude to an Atlantic area in which Europe would lose personality.

    2. A closer association between the Common Market and the European Free Trade Association could be formed. Such an association is "provided for in the Treaty of Rome and should multiply and help the economic relations of the contracting parties."

    3. Finally, Great Britain could wait until she achieves the "profound

---

[15] May 17, 1967, p. 46.
[16] *U. S. News and World Report*, May 15, 1967, p. 52.

economic and political transformation which would allow her to join the six continentals."

De Gaulle left little doubt concerning his preference for the third alternative. According to Charles Hargrove writing from Paris May 16, 1967:

> There was only a very small qualification to the new "No" of General de Gaulle. That involved a "historic" conversion on Britain's part which she had obviously not accomplished, and which, he clearly implied, would not take place for many a year—assuredly not in his own lifetime.[17]

What were the arguments advanced by General de Gaulle to support this conclusion:

1. "England, which is not a continental country, which because of the Commonwealth and its own island status has faraway commitments, and which is tied to the United States by all sorts of special agreements, could not merge into a community of fixed dimensions and rigorous rules" (insularity and Trojan Horse arguments). De Gaulle makes no acknowledgment of the changes of the last four years. His remarks at this point are a parroting of those of 1963. This reiteration of "special" ties and "special" relationships seems to be nothing more than a bit of semantic felicity for which de Gaulle has become quite well known.

2. Concerning agriculture, if England is allowed to enter under the present conditions, her balance of payments will collapse. If the treaty is changed, it would disrupt the equilibrium of the entire Common Market (agriculture argument). This argument completely isolates itself from Britain's bargaining position which is to accept the common agricultural policy and ask only for the transitional period that the founder-members asked for themselves.

3. De Gaulle advances a new economic argument concerning the position of the pound on the world market and particularly its status as a reserve currency. As in the other arguments, no specific proof was advanced and Wilson's carefully structured and documented arguments were not acknowledged. This economic argument comes at a time when Britain, according to her ministers, has a healthy balance of payments and the pound has been supporting the franc in the international monetary market for weeks.

Thus, I would conclude that the most distinguishing characteristic of General Charles de Gaulle's rhetoric of May 16, 1967 is its insularity. It is rhetoric in a vacuum: isolated from the changes that have occurred in the last four years, isolated from the arguments advanced by the government of Harold Wilson, and even isolated in the scope of its intended audience.

De Gaulle concluded his May 16th speech with hope for Great Britain's "historic transformation." Wilson concluded his speech with hope for a new "outward looking unity." After de Gaulle's pronouncement, Wilson emphasized his hope with these words:

> Change, industrial and political, is the nature of things and is a necessary condition of progress. Those who resist change do so at their own peril. I believe there can be no future for those who seek to pull the blankets more tightly over their heads.[18]

Perhaps the historic transformation occurred while some interested parties had the blankets over their heads. The question remains: Who's insular now?

---

[17] P. 1.
[18] *New York Times*, May 18, 1967, p. 18.

A DEBATE ON THE "DEATH-OF-GOD"

Michael R. Hagan *

I commented recently to a class that I considered absurd the notion of some people that they should not discuss religion or politics with others because the subjects are too controversial. A student put the point better than I had when he responded, "Religion and politics? What else is worth talking about?"

That we consider religion and politics among the most controversial of subjects suggests that they may be the ones most open to debate. Political debate is well known, but, except in reasonably specialized circles, religious debate is less so. So occasional, and perhaps growing, interest in public encounters between proponents of different religious persuasions is refreshing to see.

One such confrontation took place February, 1967, on the campus of the University of Chicago in a debate sponsored by the University's chapter of Inter-Varsity Christian Fellowship. There Thomas J. J. Altizer, theologian from Emory University and leading spokesman of the "Death-of-God" theology, defended his views against John Warwick Montgomery of Trinity Evangelical Divinity School.[1] An audience of 2,000 filled Rockefeller Chapel on the University campus and many would-be listeners were turned away.

The debate consisted of a thirty-minute opening speech by each participant and an hour-long exchange of comments in answer to questions from the audience. The response of the audience was enthusiastic, especially during the questioning period.

The opening statements were reasonably technical in nature, though quite different one from the other. Altizer's speech, delivered without notes or documentation, was a summary of his own position, a summary Montgomery later hailed as "succinct" and "clean-cut." It explained the theological position of "Christian atheism," the belief that God has ceased to be God, has emptied Himself of His transcendence and become totally immanent in Christ, and is now infusing into the whole world His transforming life.

Montgomery's speech was not a statement of a personal credo, as was Altizer's, but was direct refutation of his opponent's position, advancing the speaker's own beliefs only as they contrasted with Altizer's. Filled with documentation and anecdotes, it was at time biting in tone. While Altizer's presentation was extemporaneous, Montgomery's was read from a manuscript prepared in advance of the debate. In contrast to Altizer's deliberate delivery, Montgomery had to rush to squeeze in two-thirds of his prepared statement.

Though the opening statements made clear that the two men disagreed substantially, the sharpest differences occurred during the questioning

* Mr. Hagan is Acting Assistant Professor of Speech at the University of Washington.
[1] Transcripts and tape recordings of the debate are available from Inter-Varsity Press, Chicago, Illinois 60606. Quotations in this article are based upon the transcript, The Altizer-Montgomery Dialogue, copyright 1967 by Inter-Varsity Christian Fellowship, as corrected by reference to the recording. Quoted by permission.

period. Montgomery took the offensive during the latter half of the debate. In the exchanges during the questioning period, Montgomery incorporated into about half of his seventy or more statements questions directed to Altizer, and in many more made comments designed to challenge his opponent. Altizer, in contrast, spent most of his time answering Montgomery's challenges and clarifying his own position. While he did make some counter-challenges, Altizer initiated few of his own and asked only a handful of questions of his antagonist. Altizer certainly was not cowed by the barrage of questions, though he was a bit annoyed by some queries he considered irrelevant or based on misunderstanding of his position, but he was on the defensive much of the time.

The character of the exchange between the two men is indicated in the following excerpt:

A/ We understand the incarnation primarily not on the basis of deductions from the New Testament, but rather on the basis of an encounter with an understanding of the Word which is present in our midst in our flesh.

M/ There's an article by philosopher Kai Nielsen which was reprinted in *New Theology* No. I titled "Can Faith Validate God-Talk?" The essence of this article is that anybody who speaks about an encounter with something has a responsibility to make sure that he is encountering something other than his own innards. Now what I want to know is why this is an encounter with a Word?

A/ If the Word isn't present in our flesh, then it's nowhere.

M/ Well, why is it present in our flesh and not present nowhere?

A/ That is the essence of faith, that the Word is here and now in us redemptively as a source of life.

M/ Let me present you with another faith position. This has to do with a little green man who is eating toasted cheese sandwiches and is sitting on a planet exactly two miles out of the range of the best telescope on earth. He is a figure who loves us, and particularly if we eat toasted cheese sandwiches. And he has a nasty habit of moving out of the range of the telescope as they increase their range. Now, I believe in this, you see, I believe in this. How does this differ from your claim that you're having some sort of encounter with a kenotic Word?

A/ The decisive criterion is, Can you speak of it?

M/ I've just spoken of it.

A/ Oh no, that's not speech, that's gibberish.

M/ The thing that you don't seem to realize is that what you're saying is regarded as gibberish in the exact same sense because you have absolutely no criteria whatever for affirming that you're having an encounter with any Word. You've cut yourself off from any kind of criteria. Why not an encounter with bloop or gleep?[2]

Quite clear here is the slashing nature of Montgomery's attack and the biting nature of comments by both men. Montgomery's effort at many points, as in the case of the god who loves toasted cheese sandwiches, was to reduce Altizer's position to an apparent absurdity.

While he spent the bulk of his time challenging the basis of Altizer's arguments, Montgomery did not confine all of his comments to refutation. He interspersed his attacks with positive declaration of his more orthodox view of Christianity. For example, to a question as to how one can know a historical figure such as Christ or Caesar who has died in space and time, Montgomery responded:

---

[2] *The Altizer-Montgomery Dialogue,* pp. 66–68.

We come to know an historical figure personally as we come to know that historical figure objectively. Not the other way around. Anybody who tries to set personal knowledge over against objective knowledge is doomed to solipsism, and this is evident within the New Testament itself. For example, when John the Baptist was finding difficulty in retaining his commitment to Christ, being in the hoosegow, he sent his disciples to Jesus and said, "Are you the one who was supposed to come or should we look for another?" Jesus said, "Go back and tell John the things that you have heard and seen, that the dead are raised, that the blind receive their sight, that the gospel is preached," and so on. The point is that in order for John's personal commitment to remain as it ought to be, it was necessary for the personal commitment to be grounded referentially. And the great mistake of historiographers such as [Wilhelm] Dilthey is that they attempt to impart some kind of knowledge by participation which does not take seriously the objectivity of historical facts. If you want to find out about Jesus personally, the way to do it is to go to the primary historical records. Don't go to Altizer's books, don't go to Montgomery's books, go to the books that were written by people who had personal and direct contact with Christ. That's the way to find out what the Christian faith is all about, and to find out what that magnificent personal encounter with Christ can mean.[3]

As is clear from the above excerpts, the crucial issue in the debate became, which theology has the sounder objective or rational basis? Early in the debate, Altizer characterized his own position as "a confession of faith. It is in no sense a rational statement; certainly not a logical deduction."[4] And on that ground Montgomery attacked his opponent's views. Montgomery argued for the validity of the New Testament documents as an objective basis for religious commitment and made clear that, at least in this encounter, Altizer had nothing better to offer as an alternative. When Altizer did offer objective evidence for his position, such as in references to the biblical criticism of Rudolph Bultmann, Montgomery was able to parry his comments and thus keep the advantage in the debate. No matter what he may have thought of the Bible, any good debate judge would have seen that, at least in the context of this debate, the Bible is superior as evidence to what seemed to be only Altizer's subjective preferences. It may seem ironic to some that the evangelical position, itself often assailed for lacking objective proof, should come off the better when compared with Altizer's theology which claims to be more modern.

Some may feel that Altizer's position was at an unfair disadvantage, that its subjective nature could not be communicated adequately in a formal debate where the basis of decision traditionally is reasonable discourse and objective evidence. If so, Altizer was responsible for advancing his views in a situation which almost necessarily prejudiced his listeners against his approach, or for not providing them with an adequate alternative basis for judging his ideas. As it was, he tried to find a middle road and defend a theology which is subjectively based in an objective manner. The result was that neither the objective nor the subjective element of his communication was convincing. In fact, to try to substantiate a subjective position in such a manner may well have been inherently inconsistent.

---

[3] *Ibid.*, pp. 76–77.
[4] *Ibid.*, p. 10.

Montgomery's arguments were by no means flawless. He was especially guilty of allowing his *reductio ad absurdum* to become *argumentum ad hominem*, such as when he called upon Altizer to do as much as Christ and rise from the dead before founding his own religion.[5] But if the criterion for judgment of a debate is still to be the rational and objective basis of the arguments presented—and I see nothing in the Altizer-Montgomery dialogue to change that presumption—it is only fitting that the audience appeared to consider Montgomery the "winner." And the very problem Altizer faced in the debate may be the reason *Christianity Today* commented after the encounter that in theological circles "the death-of-God stir has passed like an overnight storm, and . . . it may soon be forgotten."[6]

---

[5] *Ibid.*, pp. 56 and 73.
[6] "The Waning Death-of-God Tumult," *Christianity Today,* II (May 26, 1966), 16.

BLACK POWER BENDS MARTIN LUTHER KING

ROBERT L. SCOTT*

The Meredith March in Mississippi, June, 1966, occasioned the confrontation of the slogans "Freedom Now" and "Black Power." In his most recent book, Martin Luther King, Jr., presents a dramatic account of the struggle among the organizations that took over the march after James Meredith was wounded by a shotgun blast. From the beginning, King testifies, he sensed a tension, an antagonism to white participation in the march, that he had not experienced during previous civil rights actions. At Greenwood, Mississippi, "SNCC country," Stokely Carmichael brought the Black Power chant into the open. Later at a conference of leaders to discuss the internal tensions, and especially the new slogan, King reports:

> Stokely and Floyd [McKissick of CORE] remained adamant, and Stokely concluded by saying, with candor, "Martin, I deliberately decided to raise this issue on the march in order to give it a national forum, and force you to take a stand for Black Power."
> I laughed. "I have been used before," I said to Stokely. "One more time won't hurt."
> The meeting ended with the SCLC staff members still agreeing with me that the slogan was unfortunate and would only divert attention from the evils of Mississippi, while most CORE and SNCC staff members joined Stokely and Floyd in insisting that it be projected nationally. In a final attempt to maintain unity I suggested that we compromise by not chanting either "Black Power" or "Freedom Now" for the rest of the march.[1]

King's account of what occurred and his discussion of the significance of the slogan are credible. His book, appearing a year later, must have been written so close to the genesis of the debate that it can be considered part of the event, not later wishful thinking. Furthermore, King's public statements during and since the summer of 1966 are consistent with what he says in the book.

On one judgment few are likely to disagree with Dr. King. The effort to keep the internal controversy from distracting attention from the questions of civil rights in Mississippi was not successful. "But while the chant died out," King writes, "the press kept the debate going. News stories now centered, not on the injustices of Mississippi, but on the apparent ideological division in the civil rights movement."[2] Every newspaper and popular magazine had features on Black Power, usually with sides drawn pro and con from among civil rights organizations and leaders.[3] Martin Luther King was consistently presented as being against Black Power; that he symbolizes passive resistance helped translate the issue into violence versus non-violence. Anyone studying the evidence

---

* Mr. Scott is Professor of Speech, Communication, and Theatre Arts at the University of Minnesota.
[1] Where Do We Go From Here: Chaos or Community? (New York: Harper & Row, 1967), pp. 31–32.
[2] Ibid., p. 32.
[3] See, e.g., "Negro Leaders Dividing—The Effect," U. S. News and World Report, July 18, 1966, pp. 31–34.

closely might question the propensity of the press to simplify the issue by enlisting King against Black Power, but no one can doubt that he was deeply troubled, and that while he was by no means as severe in his denunciations as was Roy Wilkins of the NAACP,[4] he believed the slogan would do more harm than good for the Negro.

Debaters, of course, seek to change the responses characteristic of their audiences. Participating in debate, however, may generate forces that will modify the participant as well. He may be brought to recognize limitations in his own position as he seeks to defend it against criticism. His recognition may stem both from arguments brought to bear by those who oppose him and from his own examination of his commitments as he finds himself pressing them on others. If he would appeal to an audience, the response tendencies which the debater must take into account will make the audience not merely a passive body to be shaped but an active force in shaping the discourse.

King's position on Black Power is an outgrowth of give and take with others within his own organization, the Southern Christian Leadership Conference—the parent of the Student Nonviolent Coordinating Committee, and with leaders of other organizations dedicated to civil rights; he has been pressed in scores of news conferences, radio and television programs, and public forums to denounce or defend Black Power. In such circumstances it is not surprising that Dr. King's voice has begun to sound some fresh notes.

In the decade following the Montgomery bus boycott, Martin Luther King became a symbol of passive resistance. Not only his ends but his means engendered controversy. Those who opposed equal rights for Negroes found his means difficult to resist. Peaceful demonstration and quiet practice of civil rights could only be countered by actions that dramatized the truth of the charges that King and his followers brought to bear. Those who stood for equal rights saw that King's means were consistent with his ends and honored him for setting an example of the strength of forbearance in the presence of evil.

King's methods have been important to him; he discussed them often, both inside "the movement" and with groups outside. To an organization of Presbyterian ministers and laymen called the Fellowship of the Concerned, he said in 1961,

> We cannot believe . . . the idea that the end justifies the means because the end is pre-existent in the means. So the idea of non-violent resistance . . . is the philosophy which says that the means must be as pure as the end, that in the long run of history, immoral destructive means cannot bring about moral and constructive ends.[5]

In the sparsely furnished office of the man who was awarded the Nobel Peace Prize in 1964, a picture of Mohandas Gandhi testifies silently to King's indebtedness; he is not apt to forget his debt nor abandon the lesson he has striven so valiantly to teach others.

---

[4] *Ibid.*, p. 34. Wilkins denounced the idea of Black Power vigorously in his address to the NAACP convention in Los Angeles. See *New York Times*, July 6, 1966, p. 14, for excerpts.

[5] "Love, Law, and Civil Disobedience," in *The Rhetoric of Racial Revolt*, ed., Roy L. Hill (Denver, Colorado: The Golden Bell Press, 1964), p. 347.

But King's ends and his means have been subjected to ridicule by the advocates of a new Negro militancy under the banner of Black Power.[6] Freedom Now has taken on a hollow ring in the face of token integration. The end of integration itself has been argued as suspect by Stokely Carmichael who pictures it as siphoning off a few of the most able Negroes from the black community leaving the many remaining the poorer for their absence.[7] Again, passive resistance, always difficult to practice, becomes more difficult as the militants remind Negroes that their passivity has always been praised as a virtue by white supremists: "We feel that integration is irrelevant; it is just a substitute for white supremacy. We have got to go after political power," Carmichael argues.[8] Some Negroes listened and at least applauded approval as H. Rap Brown went from city to city apparently fanning the fires of violence during the summer of 1967. "Stop looting and start shooting," newspapers reported him shouting to a crowd from atop a theater in riot-scarred Detroit. "The white man has declared war. We're in a rebellion."[9]

The immediate impact of Black Power on Martin Luther King is not difficult to discern. Part of the "white backlash" was a dwindling of contributions to the civil rights movement.[10] Apparently anticipating the problem, in July, 1966, the SCLC sent a letter over Dr. King's signature to its list of supporters. It began, "This letter is not a fund appeal." King labeled the Black Power slogan as "an unwise choice at the outset" with "violent connotations" that have become injurious. After re-affirming his own and the SCLC's continued adherence to non-violence, he asserted that among the Negroes in Mississippi and Chicago with whom he had marched that summer "over 90% of these dedicated activists remained adherents of the time tested principles of non-violence and interracial unity." Most of the letter emphasized that conditions of racial inequality that spawned the frustration of violence continue.

In a letter over his signature in October, 1966, this time a fund appeal, Dr. King again disassociated himself and "the vast majority of Negroes" from Black Power (citing as evidence "a *Newsweek* poll" [August 22, 1966, p. 34]. But he subtly exploited the threat: "Yet it would be hazardous to be complacent or smug because the appeal of extremist black power is narrow. The allure of 'Black Power' in its extremist or moderate senses springs from real, not imaginary causes." The letter pressed the miserable conditions to be dealt with, but with more emphasis on the urban ghetto than regular recipients of fund appeals from the SCLC had seen in the past. The readers were given implicit alternatives: accept the festering sores that lead to violence or support a constructive, non-violent organization. The letter concluded, "We need your support. Will you join with

---

[6] "At the CORE convention [July, 1966], middle-class Negroes were derided as 'black-power brokers,' 'handkerchief heads,' and 'Dr. Thomases' (Uncle Toms with attaché cases), and moderate Negro preachers like Dr. King were called 'chicken-eating preachers.'" *Time*, July 15, 1966, p. 16.

[7] See, e.g., "Toward Black Liberation," *Massachusetts Review*, VII (Autumn, 1966), 647.

[8] Cited in "SNCC Does Not Wish to Become a New Version of the White Man's Burden," *I. F. Stone's Weekly*, June 6, 1966, p. 3.

[9] "Brown Presses Violence Theme," *Minneapolis Star*, August 28, 1967, p. 6B.

[10] See, e.g., "A Major Turning Point Against the Negro Movement," *U. S. News and World Report*, October 3, 1966, p. 46.

those who are investing in democracy. It will yield no profit except the satisfaction of shaping a future of brotherhood, freedom and harmony."

But the impact of Black Power on Martin Luther King has been more than that of immediate rhetorical necessities, such as disassociating himself from the violence, and of opportunities, such as presenting the SCLC as an alternative. In King today there is more stress on building pragmatically economic and political strength and on using that strength, and there is a fresh emphasis on creating a sense of pride in Negro manhood. The change in direction was evident early in the furore over Black Power. A writer for *Newsweek* saw the turn taken: "Integration is out: the rallying cry for King's own campaign in Chicago is not 'integrate' but 'end slums'; the means, in effect, is Black Power without calling it that."[11]

In the year that followed the turbulent summer of 1966, Dr. King made pride and power consistent with love and non-violence. His new rhetoric is brilliantly displayed in his report to the Tenth Anniversary Convention of the Southern Christian Leadership Conference in Atlanta, Georgia, August 16, 1967.[12]

There is in this address, as one soon learns to expect in reading and listening to Dr. King, the repetitions of sound and phrase which give his speech a richly melodic quality. He begins by saying that Negroes a decade ago were "harried by day and haunted by night by a corroding sense of fear and a nagging sense of 'nobodyness.'" But pressure has caused "the sagging walls of segregation to come tumbling down" (p. 1). Throughout the opening, "ten years ago" is a refrain varied occasionally with "a decade ago." At the end of the speech, when King charges his hearers to keep their faith and renew their courage in the weary strife, "let us be dissatisfied" and finally "let us remember" and "let us realize" bring the drumbeat to his peroration (pp. 16–17).

But added to these familiar elements, to the allusions and direct references to the Bible, are echoes of the language of Black Power. Anyone who has heard and read Stokely Carmichael's angry words to white America, "I just want you to get off my back," may be jolted by King's "In short, over the last ten years, the Negro decided to straighten his back up, realizing that a man cannot ride your back unless it is bent" (p. 2). Even the black nationalism that has made common cause with revolutionaries around the world is reflected in King's "the ghetto is a domestic colony that's constantly drained without being replenished. You are always telling us to lift ourselves by our own bootstraps and yet we are being robbed every day. Put something back in the ghetto!" (p. 6).

King's speech is a report on the past programs and future plans of the SCLC; it is also a refutation of the violent implications of Black Power, an absorption of the moderate implications of Black Power, and a challenge to a broadened task for those who have identified themselves with the civil rights movement. Underneath the subtle modifications of the language and the direct argument to these ends lies a well-wrought progression of thought in which each point prepares for the one that follows.

The speech opens appropriately with the stuff of a report. King uses the occasion of the tenth anniversary to stress past accomplishment, but

---

[11] *Newsweek*, July 11, 1966, p. 31.
[12] All references will be to the official version of the speech distributed by the SCLC, 334 Auburn Avenue, N. E., Atlanta, Georgia.

the past accomplishment is focused to highlight a picture of radical change to cut some of the ground out from under the militants who have challenged King and his methods: "The courage with which [the Negro] confronted enraged mobs dissolved the stereotype of the grinning, submissive Uncle Tom. He came out of his struggle integrated only slightly in the external society, but powerfully integrated within. This was a victory that had to precede all other gains" (pp. 1–2).

Although the 1966 report had included the story of the SCLC's expansion into the northern ghettos with "Operation Breadbasket," King's 1967 speech covers the work in Chicago and Cleveland in much more detail than that in the South. Such emphasis may be explained partially by recognizing that the delegates were more than well aware of the work in the South but needed to know more of the fresh accomplishments in the North, but even so, the stress on political and economic awareness and the molding of awareness into accomplishment occupies territory that the Black Power advocates saw as largely untouched by the drive for civil rights.

To the story of accomplishment and progress echoing with overtones of power, King adds another argument preparatory to a direct attack on Black Power. Picturing a nation in which the Negro's plight has been more than economic and political exploitation but one of psychological debasement, King calls upon the listener to "upset this cultural homicide," to affirm "his own Olympian manhood," to confirm "his psychological freedom" with "a firm sense of self-esteem." In doing so he adopts a phrase which had become associated with ghetto militants, "Yes, we must stand up and say, 'I'm black and I'm beautiful! . . .'" (p. 9).[13] King had often in the past appealed to self-esteem—his Christian sense of rightness set non-violence as the goal of a strong, dedicated man. But a pride in being black puts his drive for integration on a fresh basis, a little more like Stokely Carmichael's demand for a coalition of equal groups rather than an integration of selected individuals.

The lists of active accomplishments and the strong, proud identification with being black prepare the audience for the speaker's direct attack on violence. The first step in this attack is to define "legitimate power" as "the ability to achieve purpose" (p. 10); this step echoes the report of progress and promise just completed. The next step is to face the tension between "power" and "love":

> What is needed is a realization that power without love is reckless and abusive and love without power is sentimental and anemic. Power at its best is love implementing the demands of justice, and justice at its best is power correcting everything that stands against love. And this is what we must see as we move on (p. 10).

The tension is resolved in Christian love. The failure to resolve the tension, to cry for the revenge of "destructive and conscienceless power" is associated with the abhorrent reality of white supremacy (p. 11). This appeal is familiar to King's rhetoric: we must be better than they or sink even deeper to more shameful levels.

---

[13] For an interesting account of Stokely Carmichael's use of "I am black and I am beautiful," in a speech in Tallahassee, Florida, April 16, 1967, see Elizabeth F. Phifer, "Carmichael in Tallahassee," *Southern Speech Journal*, XXXIII (Winter, 1967), 89.

After a thoroughly pragmatic attack on taking the idea of Black Power literally as revolution in America ("It is perfectly clear that a violent revolution on the part of the American blacks would find no sympathy and support from the white population and very little from the majority of the Negroes themselves" p. 13), King proposes a deeper revolution: the restructuring of American society, which he relates to the confrontation of Jesus and Nicodemus, "America, you must be born again!" (p. 16).

King recognizes the pull that radical philosophy, economic and political, has had on many bright, young Negroes growing cynical in the contradictions of American life.

> What I'm saying to you this morning is that Communism forgets that life is individual. Capitalism forgets that life is social, and the Kingdom of Brotherhood is found neither in the thesis of Communism nor the antithesis of Capitalism but in a higher synthesis. . . . Now, when I say question the whole society, it means ultimately coming to see that the problem of racism, the problem of economic exploitation, and the problem of war are all tied together. These are the triple evils that are interrelated (p. 15).

Perhaps King never believed that his fight for integration was a fight to allow Negroes to be absorbed into a corrupt society, but his struggle with Black Power has made him emphasize the need for radical change. Whether this is an old or a new insight for King, he creates of it an opportunity to make a common cause with anyone, white or black, who will recognize that poverty, war, and hatred are symptoms of deep trouble that necessitate fundamental changes. Further he reaffirms his faith in non-violent methods on the familiar ground that violence will corrupt any change it brings.

Martin Luther King's address to the Tenth Anniversary Convention of the SCLC is an impressive document. In it the speaker displays a vocabulary freshened by its confrontation with Black Power and a program with more depth and breadth than the civil rights movement had known previously.

Of course no one, including Dr. King, can be certain of the influence of Black Power on his rhetoric. The SCLC had turned northward with Operation Breadbasket before the Meredith march; whether this drive would have assumed the importance it did in his 1967 report without the evident necessity of making some sort of response to Black Power is difficult to say. Further, Dr. King was disenchanted with the Vietnam war before the outcry of the well-known Black Power advocates.

In his 1966 report to the SCLC, Dr. King said, "But before we were able to depart from the 1965 Convention, the fires of Watts began to burn and with Watts a whole new era of the civil rights struggle emerged."[14] In this earlier presidential address, King touched on Black Power several times, but in 1967 direct and indirect references to the idea fascinating many Negroes permeates his report.

No one who reads or hears King can doubt that he is being influenced by a man who is rooted deeply in strong commitments, commitments which are not apt to be sundered in the changing winds of events. Nor can one

---

[14] "President's Annual Report by Dr. Martin Luther King, Jr., President, Southern Christian Leadership Conference, Delivered in Jackson, Mississippi, August 10, 1966." [Mimeographed, SCLC].

doubt that here is a man who has exposed himself, and will expose himself, to the forces of change roaring about him. If indeed he has been bent in the debate over Black Power, bending may be a sign of strength; that which is bent may itself gain energy as a shaping force.

James Farmer, former director of CORE, writes that "the debate will rage on between cohesiveness and dispersion. Ascendancy of one camp or the other will be determined ultimately not by rhetoric, and not even by leadership, as much as by events. Events today seem to be racing to the side of the spirited new force—cohesion—and I think that is right and good for the black man at this historical juncture."[15] Farmer is right in seeing the priority of events in shaping the future and in judging that these are destined to arouse stronger feelings of community among Negroes. The question is on what terms will Negroes be cohesive? Would Farmer be able to identify the "spirited new force" at all if it were not in the process of developing some sort of recognizable character, which is about the same thing as saying if it were not being articulated by leaders.

If the next step forward for Negroes in America is to come through the development of organized political and economic power which will tend to emphasize the black community as a community, the problem of who will lead and with what philosophy is crucial. Writing in 1963, before the Black Power crisis, Martin Luther King saw the past failure of Negroes to shape and use power:

> Negroes have traditionally positioned themselves too far from the inner arena of political decision. Few other minority groups have maintained a political aloofness and a nonpartisan posture as rigidly and as long as Negroes. The Germans, Irish, Italians, and Jews, after a period of acclimatization, moved inside political formations and exercised influence. Negroes, partly by choice but substantially by exclusion, have operated outside of the political structures, functioning instead essentially as a pressure group with limited effect.[16]

The debate over Black Power has quickened King's concern for moving in directions he himself saw as necessary. Did he move soon enough? Is he moving quickly and substantially now? Does he judge the political acuity of his audience well: "By and large, Negroes remain essentially skeptical, issue-oriented, and independent-minded. Their lack of formal learning is no barrier when it comes to making intelligent choices among alternatives."[17] It is too early to answer these questions, but it is not too early to recognize that a man who has been predominant in the civil rights movement for the past decade is in the process of adapting his rhetoric to take advantage of and to modify the new force generated by an increasing awareness of the limitations of the old programs and a heady desire for exercising power as a group.

Martin Luther King, resilient and enduring, presents an insight and poses a challenge to all Americans. If America is to endure it must show itself capable of bending and shaping new ways in a new world. Some of our citizens have proved their capability to persevere and adapt in the most trying circumstances. In the rhetoric of Martin Luther King, all of us have much to heed and much to hope for.

---

[15] "Are White Liberals Obsolete in the Black Struggle?" *The Progressive*, January, 1968, p. 16.
[16] *Why We Can't Wait* (New York: Harper & Row, 1963), p. 163.
[17] *Ibid.*, p. 148.

PRESIDENT JOHNSON'S VIETNAM ADDRESS: IS A MASTERFUL POLITICAL STRATEGY NECESSARILY A GOOD SPEECH?

BERNARD L. BROCK *and* ROBERT L. SCOTT*

On March 30, 1968, when the national approval of his Presidency had dropped to 36 per cent and acceptance of his Vietnam policy had sunk to a mere 26 per cent,[1] Lyndon Baines Johnson disclosed that he would present a national radio and television address on Vietnam. In the address that followed on March 31, the President both surprised and shocked the nation. He surprised the nation because he significantly modified previous policies by announcing a bombing pause, in effect a unilateral de-escalation of the war, designed to pave the way for peace negotiations. And he shocked the nation because in the final moments of the speech he announced that he would neither seek nor accept another term as President. The shock was written on the faces of the follow-up news commentators who groped for words to respond to the announcement which had not been included in copies of the address released before delivery.

The President's message was an act upon a scene defined by the realities of a war abroad and a rapidly escalating political campaign at home. Johnson had been thoroughly identified with a war policy that argued for peace and held that it would come when aggressors from the North had been punished to a degree that would bring them to the conference table. Further, the President was assumed to be a proud man who delighted in domestic political battle and would automatically be a candidate in the fall. Unquestionably reversing these expectations was a masterful strategy directed toward an end generally agreed highly desirable—a meaningful peace. But to make maximum the impact for good, the speech itself had to make the strategy consistent with the realities as Johnson's audiences throughout the world had learned to view them. We shall discuss first the President's speech as a grand act on the world and domestic scene and then ask whether or not the speech itself met the demands of the grand strategy.

1

Any evaluation of Johnson's address needs to consider its political and military implications. At the time, the President had become both politically and militarily stymied. Politically, American policy in Vietnam had become the dominant issue in the growing Presidential campaign, and Johnson's critics, as suggested by the Gallup Poll approval of only 26 per cent, had gained the upper hand on the issue. What was the effect of Johnson's strategy in the speech? His political timing was excellent. McCarthy had just successfully challenged him in New Hampshire. The significance of McCarthy's feat was surely reflected in Robert Kennedy's decision to enter the campaign for support in the primaries. These men represented a strong threat to Johnson's leadership. They would have a difficult time gaining suf-

* *Mr. Brock is Assistant Professor of Speech, Communication, and Theatre Arts and Director of Forensics at the University of Minnesota. Mr. Scott is a Professor in the same department.*

[1] "Approval of LBJ Dips to New Low," *The Minneapolis Tribune*, March 31, 1968, sect. 1, p. 1.

ficient delegate strength to deprive Johnson of the nomination for a second term, but they could so undermine his acceptance by the people that he could not be re-elected in November. The campaign among Democrats was already broadening to the effectiveness of the President's administration in every current economic and social question as well as the war. Given that condition, President Johnson had a great deal to lose by taking part in a debate over the policies followed during his administration. He would very nearly be forced to do so if he expected to be nominated, but in doing so would increase the chances of retiring into history as a loser. Of course the address was made only two days before the Wisconsin primary to a domestic audience conscious that the public opinion polls were predicting that the President would receive only 40 per cent of the vote. The political tide at the moment seemed to be running against Johnson; the situation was ripe for some political move on his part.

The move he selected was to combine the announcement of de-escalation in Vietnam with his refusal to be a Presidential candidate in 1968. What were the effects of this well-timed political move? First, overnight he became a hero. An editorial in the *Washington Post* made a typical comment: "He has made a personal sacrifice in the name of national unity that entitles him to a very special place in the annals of American history."[2] Praise in both houses of Congress was fulsome. The credibility gap which had so long plagued the President was closed. Only a man of integrity would subordinate his own political interests to the interests of the nation. Johnson's new image could be seen in the 13 per cent increase in his popularity.[3]

A second effect was a tendency to offset the impact of the New Hampshire and, two days later, the Wisconsin primaries. Was it significant if a non-candidate lost in the primaries? Further, much of the punch was taken out of the campaigns of the Democrats who opposed the President. The drama of Senator Kennedy's entry into the campaign was eclipsed. Eugene McCarthy, who had been largely a one-issue candidate, had to start anew.

Third, and probably most important, Johnson's move placed a strong restraint on discussing Vietnam. The President had ostensibly agreed to try measures urged by his opponents while not necessarily accepting the philosophy of his critics. But who would be willing to assume the responsibility of jeopardizing the prospects of peace by attacking President Johnson while he was attempting to set up negotiations?

Finally, Johnson's strategy of withdrawing from the race while simultaneously making a peace move increased his chances of being elected if he were to become the nominee. Immediately after his announcement the mass media considered the possibility of a convention draft; several politicians urged the President to reconsider and began to talk draft. Undoubtedly, Johnson's chances of being re-elected in November would increase if he would avoid an extended debate over his Vietnam policy. In a sense if he should be drafted for candidacy, he has embarked on a political course which must redound to his credit. If the peace moves succeed or seem to be

---

[2] The editorial from the April 1, 1968 *Washington Post* was read into the *Congressional Record* of that day, 90th Cong., 2d Sess., S 3669, at the request of Senator Gale McGee of Wyoming. Comments on the speech throughout the *Record* of April 1 are well worth study.

[3] "49 Pct. Now Back LBJ's Performance," *The Minneapolis Tribune*, April 17, 1968, sect. 1, p. 1.

succeeding, he can profit from the relief which should sweep through the electorate; if they do not succeed, he can claim to have tried methods like those urged by his most effective critics and argue that his long-standing attitude toward the Vietnam war was proved correct.

As one observes the impact of the address on the nation, he must conclude that it was a masterful political strategy. At least Johnson avoids retiring a bitter loser, and he may have set the stage for remarkable nomination and election. When the events were turning against him, he was able to reverse the tide and improve his future possibilities.

However, a review of the military-diplomatic situation raises some questions about the effectiveness of the address. One must ask whether the military-diplomatic move brought the United States closer to a solution in Vietnam. Since 1965, the United States had significantly increased its participation in the war, including the extensive bombing of North Vietnam. The purpose of this escalation was to make the war too costly for North Vietnam to bear. This policy had been successful in making the war costly, but it did not prevent the North Vietnamese from escalating their participation as well. Finally, with the TET offensive, it became apparent that the United States could not win a military victory without the complete destruction of North Vietnam and most of South Vietnam. Within this setting, President Johnson unilaterally de-escalated the war even though he had previously refused to take such an action.

In assessing Johnson's bid for peace, one should point out the difficulties of making judgments in the diplomatic field. One can only observe and raise questions. The issue is further complicated because a peace bid could not be evaluated by any audience, domestic, allied, or opponent, independent of its domestic political repercussion.

Whereas the timing for the political retirement was excellent, the bombing pause was poorly timed. In some respects it was too late, while in others it was too early. It came too late to prevent Vietnam from becoming a political issue which divided both major political parties. Also, it was almost certainly too late to conclude negotiations successfully by the August conventions, and probably before the November election. The issue of timing raises the question of what the North Vietnamese would have to gain by entering into serious negotiations before January when supposedly the United States would have a new President. Wouldn't North Vietnam stall negotiations until it could sit down with a team less personally involved in the present policy than the Johnson administration? All of these observations and questions suggest that the Johnson peace bid came too late to allow him to conclude them before he left office.

Now, in what ways might the bid have been presented too early? Vietnam had become a political issue which divided the country, but the issue had not been debated sufficiently to resolve the differences in favor of a new policy for Vietnam. The quasi-moratorium on debate imposed by the peace bid came when the nation was divided. No one can now predict how this division will manifest itself later. When debate resumes, will a breakdown in negotiations result in further escalation? Will a divided nation accept a treaty as negotiated? Is it desirable for one administration to start negotiations which are probably going to be concluded by another? Behind these questions are reasons which suggest that the bid came too early, and that a new administration, either Republican or Democrat, following an election in which policy considerations figured strongly, would be in a better position to obtain a meaningful peace settlement in Vietnam.

2

Of course one may reply that we have read President Johnson's speech much too cynically. We would prefer to believe that the President was absolutely sincere in announcing his political intentions, and we hope that a meaningful peace might result somehow from the movements emanating from the speech. Our reason for believing that the speech itself was a poor start (and is a poor speech no matter what the outcome) is that it so readily allows a cynical reading while doing little to establish a firm foundation for moving ahead toward settlement of the Vietnam difficulties.

If the speech were to subordinate the President's personal career to the necessities of a hopeful future for Southeast Asia, should not his political announcement have been subordinated to the question of how we might move closer to peace? The President may be assumed to have intended to subordinate his announcement since indeed it is given as a reason consistent with the modified Vietnam policy announced earlier in the speech, but the suddenness of the brief announcement and its obvious immediate implications for the rapidly intensifying political campaign destined the statement of non-candidacy to overshadow the military and diplomatic intentions.

In a sense the President made a speech and then an announcement. The speech could well have stood without the announcement and had indeed been released without it. As it stands, the address had two centers of interest and the question which will dominate the other is left unresolved in the speech itself. The lines of argument which might have been developed to show why a President who would definitely retire in less than a year could work most meaningfully for peace are left largely undeveloped in favor of an introduction to a dramatic announcement which highlights the deep personal sacrifice of the public man, Lyndon B. Johnson.

Other choices were available to the President. He could have announced his political intentions before the speech, saying in press conference, for example, that these were closely related to new plans for Vietnam which would be developed at length in a major policy address in a few days. The policy could have been made to seem the careful consideration of a close re-evaluation on the part of the administration. Instead, no communication of extensive re-evaluation by the relevant members of the executive branch were given at the time and little has been forthcoming since. The consideration has remained largely personal and even idiosyncratic.

This evaluation is strengthened because the President did very little to indicate that the bombing pause and offer "now as in the past . . . to send its representatives to any forum, at any time, to discuss the means of bringing this ugly war to an end"[4] was indeed based on any sort of reassessment. Some forces must have brought the significant change in policy, but the domestic and foreign audiences were left to speculate on what they were.

Why the change? In some ways the President took pains to indicate no change in thinking. He reiterated the San Antonio formula early in the speech, but he had done as much dozens of times. The formula was usually interpreted as necessitating some sort of prior agreement for a bombing pause and as being consistent with the notion that North Vietnam could be brought to the peace tables only after suffering thorough punishment

---

[4] U. S., *Congressional Record*, 90th Cong., 2d Sess., April 1, 1968, S 3670. All our quotations are from this source (S 3670–S 3672). The address is also printed in the *New York Times*, April 1, 1968, and in *Vital Speeches of the Day*, April 15, 1968.

by military means. But now the President was taking unilateral action—
and he labeled it as such.

If the announcement which was certainly dramatized by being made at
the end of the address could not have been made prior to the major Vietnam
policy address, could it not have been made early in that speech as a basis
for a careful indication of reasons for a modification of policy? Johnson
only pressed points which had always been obvious: war is horrible.

> But tragically, this is also clear: many men on both sides of the struggle
> will be lost. A nation that has already suffered 20 years of warfare will
> suffer once again. Armies on both sides will take new casualties. And the
> war will go on.
> There is no need for this to be so.
> There is no need to delay the talks that could bring an end to this
> long and bloody war.
> Tonight, I renew the offer I made last August: to stop the bombard-
> ment of North Vietnam. We ask that talks begin promptly, and that
> they be serious talks on the substance of peace. We assume that during
> those talks Hanoi would not take advantage of our restraint.
> We are prepared to move immediately toward peace through negotia-
> tions.
> Tonight in the hope that this action will lead to early talks I am taking
> the first step to de-escalate the conflict. We are reducing—substantially
> reducing—the present level of hostilities.

But in the absence of military or political explanations of why he was now
willing to act unilaterally when he had previously been pressed and had
refused to make the same move, one's attention moves to the political. Thus
the question must be raised at home and in Hanoi, "Has Johnson changed
his purpose in Vietnam?" The address answers this question when the
President stated:

> But if peace does not come now through negotiations, it will come
> when Hanoi understands that our common resolve is unshakeable and our
> common strength is inevitable.

And later when he added:

> That what we are doing now, in Vietnam, is vital not only to the
> security of Asia, but to our own security. Surely we have treaties which
> we must respect, and commitments we must keep. Resolutions of Con-
> gress [Tonkin Gulf Resolution] testify to the need to resist aggression in
> Southeast Asia.

One recognizes that the President could not have deviated too much from
his previous statements, or he would undermine his ability to negotiate. But
at the same time Hanoi must wonder whether the peace bid was primarily
a strategy to improve his position at home rather than an indication that he
would be willing to negotiate meaningfully, from their point of view, in
Vietnam. In the absence of some indications of sound reasons for seeing a
fresh basis for negotiations, Hanoi could, on the other hand, believe that
unstated weaknesses, hinted at in the President's talk of needed unity and
tax measures to maintain economic strength, were bringing Johnson to
desperate measures. If so, they could either exploit those weaknesses in a
conference or delay a conference to allow a serious situation to worsen.

Assuming that President Johnson was sincerely motivated in stepping out
of contention for another term of office to make maximum his potential role
in bringing about peace, we can conclude that although his address was a
bold, dramatic act vividly highlighted by the domestic and world scene,
the details of the speech itself are not consistent with the demands of the

circumstances. It is at best a mediocre speech, even though hopefully it may initiate a conference that will lead to a meaningful peace.

Although firm conclusions about the eventual outcome cannot now be drawn, two questions should be stressed: "What form will the existing divisions in domestic opinion over Vietnam take?" "What do the North Vietnamese have to gain by starting serious negotiations now instead of stalling until a new administration is inaugurated?"

Presently, both sides are sparring over starting negotiations. These overtures are a direct result of Johnson's address, and they may pave the way for a new President to settle the war and preside over another stage in the thawing of the Cold War. But in the meantime the war in Vietnam has not changed significantly, although President Johnson seems to have improved his political image through masterful use of personal sacrifice.

SENATE VIETNAM DEBATE—MARCH 7, 1968

PETER E. KANE*

Congressional debate in both the Senate and House of Representatives is generally a formalized ritual. Typically it would consist of a series of statements inserted into the *Congressional Record* or read in an almost empty chamber. This pattern of debate has led some advocates of Congressional reform to suggest that in the interest of efficiency all live debate be discontinued. Such action would eliminate the only national forum for the presentation and consideration of views on major issues regardless of how infrequently that forum is used. The magnitude of such a loss was clearly seen in the Senate debate of March 7, 1968, on United States policy in Vietnam. While this rare three-hour extemporaneous debate was reported by the news media, these reports were fragmentary and often a reflection of the ornithological coloration of the reporting agency rather than what really happened. It is the purpose of this report to present the event in detail and as objectively as possible.

The business before the Senate on March 7 was HR 2516, the 1968 Civil Rights Bill. At this time the Senate was proceeding under the rules of cloture. These rules allow each Senator to speak for only one hour until after a final vote on this measure. No Senator could yield any of his time to another Senator, and thus, except for questions, no Senator could yield to another while retaining the floor. The effect of the rules was that the time taken by each Senator to discuss Vietnam was charged to the time remaining of his hour to debate HR 2516. In spite of the tendency of the cloture rules to discourage all but those feeling most strongly on the issue to speak, one-fourth of the total Senate membership representing twenty-three states did participate.

The controversy began immediately after a close vote on a housing amendment to the Civil Rights Bill offered by Senator Robert Byrd of West Virginia. Senator J. William Fulbright took five minutes of his time for HR 2516 to make a few remarks about Vietnam.

> I do not wish to detain the Senate too long, but I wish to raise an issue. While it is not directly related to the business now before the Senate, I believe it is indirectly related to it. . . .
>
> There are rumors—or more than rumors—I am quite certain from the news that has come to us through the press and elsewhere, that very significant decisions are being considered by the executive branch of our Government, decisions involving a major new buildup of American forces in Vietnam—not only a buildup of troops, but also there is the possibility of the extension of the war beyond the geographical limits of Vietnam.
>
> I believe these pending decisions raise a basic and most important constitutional issue which must concern every Member of this body, regardless of whether he supports or disagrees with the administration's war policy. This issue is the authority of the administration to expand the war without the consent of Congress and without any debate or consideration by Congress.
>
> . . . .
>
> Insofar as the consent of this body is said to derive from the Gulf of Tonkin resolution, it can be said that that resolution, like any contract based on misrepresentation is null and void. . . .[1]

---

* Mr. Kane is Assistant Professor of Speech at Harpur College, State University of New York at Binghamton and Faculty Sponsor of the DSR-TKA chapter there.
[1] U. S., *Congressional Record*, 90th Cong., 2d Sess., March 7, 1968, S 2360.

When Fulbright finished his own statement he yielded the floor to several other Senators to make remarks on their own time. While there was some critical comment on administration policy, most speakers directed their main attention to the central point of Fulbright's statement. For example, Senator Mark Hatfield of Oregon observed,

> I think the question is not whether we dissent from or assent to the present war policy as much as it is a question of what is the proper role that we in Congress should play in the general warmaking policies of our country. . . .
>
> . . . .
>
> Congress must be a full, participating partner in this particular warmaking policy that the President has embarked upon.[2]

Senator Frank Church of Idaho added,

> The Constitution vests in Congress a fundamental responsibility in the matter of war and peace. We have abdicated that responsibility in recent years. The last two wars have been Presidential wars.
>
> Now we are at a critical point in determining whether this war shall continue to be a limited engagement or whether it is going to spread into a general engagement on the Asian mainland.
>
> This is the time to reassert our prerogative, to insist upon full congressional participation in that decision. This is the time.[3]

During the remarks of Senator Robert Kennedy of New York the tone of the debate changed. He began with comment on the Constitutional question and ended by dealing with some emotion with some of the substantive elements of the administration's policy.

> I think it would be a mistake for the executive branch and for the President to take a step toward escalation of the conflict in the next several weeks without having the support and understanding of the Senate, and of the American people.
>
> . . . .
>
> Moreover, there is a question of our moral responsibility. Are we like the God of the Old Testament that we can decide, in Washington, D.C., what cities, what towns, what hamlets in Vietnam are going to be destroyed?
>
> . . . .
>
> I would like to know what the people of South Vietnam are going to be willing to do themselves.
>
> If we are going to draft American troops of 18 and 19 years of age and send them to Khe Sanh, Con Thien, and on the border of the demilitarized zone, are we also going to say—as we now are doing—that the people of South Vietnam do not have to draft their own 18-year-old and 19-year-old boys?[4]

After calling on a half-dozen Senators who shared his views Fulbright yielded to Senator John Tower of Texas resulting in the following exchange and statement:

> The implication has been made that we have suffered a series of very great defeats in South Vietnam. I do not accept that thesis. I am not saying that we have accomplished a great deal in that unhappy land in the last 6 weeks.
>
> Mr. FULBRIGHT. . . . If we did not suffer any defeat or difficulty, why is there a request for 200,000 additional troops?
>
> Mr. TOWER. Because now the administration is doing what a number

---

[2] *Ibid.*, S 2362.
[3] *Ibid.*, S 2363.
[4] *Ibid.*, S 2363-S 2364.

of us have been saying for 2½ years—that you cannot win a war by a
gradual response of gradualism; that the only way to achieve military
victory is through military power, massive air and sea superiority, to
achieve the objective at the earliest possible time, with the maximum of
impact.

. . . .

. . . [The enemy] has established his infrastructures clandestinely in
most of the underdeveloped countries of this world; and every time this
clandestine infrastructure surfaces and starts a guerrilla war, there are
too many people in this country who say it is just a little old domestic
revolution.

Mr. President, it is no such thing. . . .

If we abandon Vietnam, then, of course, we abandon Laos as well, and
Cambodia, and then Thailand. What are we going to do about Thailand?
There is a Communist underground organization mounting terrorist attacks against the people in Thailand, and North Vietnamese guerrillas are
deeply involved.

. . . .

The late Adlai Stevenson defended our position in South-East Asia. He
said that we cannot allow them to continue opening door after door
that will result in the ultimate conflagration.[5]

In his statement, the only extended comment by a "hawk," Senator
Tower made several of the points widely used to justify an aggressive policy
in Vietnam. He did not speak to Fulbright's main question of the role of
Congress in Vietnam policy decisions.

By the time Senator Tower had concluded, the *Record* indicates that
several Senators were seeking to be recognized. Fulbright, who still held
the floor, yielded in turn to Senators Vance Hartke of Indiana, Joseph
Tydings of Maryland, and Gaylord Nelson of Wisconsin—all in general
agreement with Fulbright's Vietnam position. In response to Senator
Nelson's comments Fulbright expanded upon his original criticism of the
Gulf of Tonkin resolution.

I believe the Senator [Nelson] is speaking of a debate on August 7,
1964. Of course, I was relying upon the truthfulness of the Secretary
of State, the Secretary of Defense, and the Chairman of the Joint Chiefs.
At that time I was not very experienced in dealing with these gentlemen,
and I believed everything they told us—not only with respect to the facts
but also as to their interpretation of their policy.

I also believed the President of the United States when he said that his
purpose was not to fight a war in Asia with American boys. I have his
exact statement in my notes.[6]

This statement clearly shows how far the debate had moved in a little less
than two hours from the original point—Congress' role in Vietnam policy-
making. Rather Fulbright modified his original veiled charge of misrepre-
sentation to a fairly explicit charge that the President and his leading
cabinet officers had lied regarding the Tonkin Gulf resolution.

These comments were followed by an extended, noisy, and bitter parliamentary dispute. The source of antagonism was threefold. First, there
was resentment at Fulbright's refusal to allow his opponents to speak by
failing to yield to them. The propriety of the Senator's procedure was challenged by Senators John Stennis of Mississippi, Norris Cotton of New
Hampshire, Albert Gore of Tennessee, and Gordon Allott of Colorado. The
point which was finally established was that a Senator could not yield to

[5] *Ibid.*, S 2364-S 2366.
[6] *Ibid.*, S 2368.

another Senator under cloture and still retain the floor except for the purpose of being asked a question. The statements by other Senators had clearly not been questions. The result of this parliamentary point was that Senator Fulbright was forced to conclude his own remarks and yield the floor.

Second, because the Vietnam question had been raised while the Senate was operating under the rules of cloture, a complete exchange of views was impossible. Many of the Senators who opposed Fulbright's views were actively involved in the debate on the Civil Rights Bill and reluctant to use their time to discuss anything other than the HR 2516 and its pending amendments. After trying unsuccessfully for more than an hour Senator Frank Lausche of Ohio finally obtained the floor and expressed the displeasure with the timing of the debate.

> I suggest to the chairman of the Committee on Foreign Relations that instead of talking continuously on this subject, he introduce a resolution to the Senate—one, to repeal the Gulf of Tonkin resolution; two, if he does not want to do that, then a resolution to adopt the Gavin enclave recommendation; and three, if he does not want to do either of the first two, then to present a resolution to declare that we pull out of South Vietnam and raise the white flag of surrender.[7]

The third source of antagonism was Senator Fulbright's attack on the integrity of the President and his Cabinet Secretaries Dean Rusk and Robert McNamara. After Fulbright had been forced to give up the floor, the Senate Majority Leader, Mike Mansfield of Montana, attempted to smooth over this matter by in effect retracting Fulbright's charge.

> I think it is fair to say that regardless of how one feels about the situation in Vietnam, in Southeast Asia, and in Korea, the President has tried hard and vigorously and consistently to find a way to the negotiating table, to the end that an honorable truce could be achieved and an honorable settlement effected.
>
> One may disagree with his San Antonio formula, or with his Johns Hopkins speech, but I hope Senators will not impugn his motives; and to the best of my knowledge, no one in this Chamber has.
>
> . . . .
>
> We cannot recall the Gulf of Tonkin resolution. If I knew then what I know today, I would have voted against it. However, I cannot operate on hindsight. I voted for the Gulf of Tonkin resolution.
>
> Those witnesses who appeared before the Foreign Relations Committee were, in my opinion, honest and candid on the basis of the information at their disposal. And, as far as McNamara was concerned when he appeared some days ago before our committee in his farewell appearance, I think he was candid and honest in what he had to say about the intelligence activities of one or both of these destroyers.[8]

With the papering-over of the last area of antagonism the debate concluded on a new point which sprang directly from the antagonism which had been created. Senator George McGovern of South Dakota noted the value of free expression of dissent and was critical of the advertising used to support President Johnson's election campaign in New Hampshire.

> Those are the tactics of Hitler's Germany and Stalin's Russia. Those are the tactics that would silence free and open discussion of honest differences of opinion.
>
> . . . .
>
> . . . I think the point made by the Senator from Montana is well taken that it does not really require very much courage or patriotism to stand

---

[7] *Ibid.*, S 2378
[8] *Ibid.*, S 2375-S 2376.

on the floor of the Senate and cheer our troops on to their deaths. Our responsibility would be abandoned by that kind of blind endorsement of a policy that we believe to be mistaken and not in the national interest.[9]

Senator Gore concluded the debate by quoting at length from Patrick Henry's famous "Liberty or Death" speech and adding,

> This dilemma is as old as our Republic. The dilemma is whether, in certain situations, patriotism demands that men hold their tongues or speak their minds; whether the true patriot, who questions the course of action his government is taking, should remain silent and thus by his silence give his assent to the conduct and policies of his government or should instead, in voice challenge the wisdom of his leaders.
>
> I believe, Mr. President, that a U.S. Senator not only has a right to express his dissent but a duty to do so, and the greater the cause, the greater the duty. It will be a lamentable day, indeed, when U.S. Senators refrain from criticizing or questioning the policies of our Government because of the fear that to do so will bring upon them the opprobrium, the accusation, the insinuation or the question of being unpatriotic. This shall not be. And, as Patrick Henry noted, the more important the subject, the freer—the more outspoken—should be the debate.[10]

In summary, the Vietnam debate in the Senate on March 7, 1968, was a most remarkable event. While the Senate was debating under cloture the Civil Rights Bill of 1968 (HR 2516), Senator Fulbright took the floor to request greater Congressional participation in Vietnam decision-making. Several other Senators supported his request and led the discussion into specific criticism of President Johnson's policies. The timing of these remarks, the manner in which Fulbright stifled dissent, and the perceived intemperance with which charges against the administration came to be stated caused an antagonistic reaction among many Senators who did not share Fulbright's Vietnam views. After an attempt to sooth ruffled feelings, a counter reaction resulted in comments regarding the importance of free expression of dissenting views.

The objection might be raised that this Vietnam debate violated the Senate's rule of germaneness in that it had nothing to do with civil rights. However, others might argue that Vietnam affects all aspects of American life. As Senator Joseph Clark of Pennsylvania put it,

> Vietnam is a cancer which is devouring our youth, our morals, our national wealth, and the energies of our leadership. The casualty list from this war only begins on the battlefield. As victims, we must also count the programs of the Great Society, the balance of payments, a sound budget, a stable dollar, the world's good will, detente with the Soviet Union, and hopes for a durable world peace. The toll of this war can never be measured in dollars spent—they are only the tip of a vast iceberg whose bulk can never be accurately measured.[11]

One immediate evaluation of this debate was made by Senator McGovern who said, "I wish to express my appreciation as a Member of the Senate and as a citizen of this country for what I regard as possibly the most significant discussion held on the Senate floor in many years."[12] Even if McGovern's evaluation is only partially correct, continuation of Congressional floor debate had been justified.

---

[9] *Ibid.*, S 2377–S 2378.

[10] *Ibid.*, S 2382.

[11] *Ibid.*, S 2379.

[12] *Ibid.*, S 2377.

ANTI-WAR RHETORIC AND THE PARIS PEACE TALKS

DAVID H. SMITH

Throughout their analysis of President Johnson's Vietnam Address in the May *Speaker and Gavel* Brock and Scott consider its impact on the possibility of serious negotiations to end the Vietnam war. While we now know that that speech did ultimately lead to the current Paris talks, some question remains as to whether those talks can be termed "serious" negotiation. Brock and Scott argue that North Vietnam would be likely to stall any negotiations until after the inauguration of a new United States administration. The question of what constitutes a serious bargaining strategy aside, their prediction seems to have been accurate. Few Americans are likely to view the Paris activities as progress toward settlement. Whether or not this will change dramatically in January is, of course, another question.

My purpose here is not to examine the Brock and Scott article point by point. I propose, rather, to deal with the assumption, only indirectly stated in their article, that there is a relationship between political rhetoric in the United States and the likelihood of a negotiated settlement in Southeast Asia. I will consider the strategic nature of negotiation, the relevance of typical American assumptions about negotiation, and, finally, the impact of anti-war rhetoric on the Paris negotiations.

Negotiation is, first of all, a decision-making system based on tactics. The element of conflict which is part of the relationship between the parties requires the implementation of strategies designed to exact the most favorable terms from one's opponent with the least cost to oneself. The sole constraint on the use of tactics is the possible failure of the parties to reach a mutually acceptable settlement, thus forfeiting the advantages of settlement and continuing the costs of the unsettled relationship.

Two important strategic problems face the negotiator: 1. Shall he invoke a "hard" or "soft" bargaining strategy? 2. How can he obtain and use information about minimum dispositions?

The first strategic problem relates to how conciliatory or adamant his pose will be. If the negotiator chooses a "hard" strategy, he will make large demands very firmly, be quite unyielding and bring great pressure to bear on his opponent. In so doing he increases his chances for a more favorable settlement, but he risks a greater chance that his opponent will cease to bargain and become willing to endure the costs of no settlement. If he chooses the "soft" strategy, he places a high value on achieving agreement and on developing alternative solutions which are not initially apparent. Since the soft strategy emphasizes obtaining agreement rather than specific demands, it leaves the negotiator vulnerable. If one party chooses a hard strategy and the second a soft strategy, the first party enjoys a large advantage, gaining the benefit of the hard strategy without its risk. The soft strategy can succeed only if both parties use it; but if one thinks his opponent may use a soft strategy, then the hard approach becomes the most advantageous tactic. If, on the other hand, one is not sure his opponent will use a soft strategy, one cannot afford to chance a soft approach himself. The result is a virtual prisoner's dilemma. The hard strategy is overwhelmingly the

---

Dr. Smith is an assistant professor in the Department of Speech, Communication, and Theatre Arts at the University of Minnesota.

more attractive tactic.[1] Only in the presence of considerable trust or in the face of horrendous consequence such as nuclear war can soft strategies be employed.

The second strategic problem involves the minimum disposition, the least favorable settlement a party is willing to accept. A party will prefer not to agree rather than settle on terms less favorable than his minimum disposition. Since the most either party can attain is a settlement which is identical with his opponent's minimum disposition, information as to what constitutes the opponent's minimum disposition is of great strategic value. If the first party can determine what terms comprise the least favorable settlement the second will accept, the first can aim his hard tactics at those terms, again confident that he has lessened the risk of no settlement inherent in the hard strategy. At the same time as he attempts to determine his opponent's minimum disposition, however, the negotiator must take care not to reveal his own. As a result the claims and demands of negotiating parties are frequently distorted to obscure rather than reveal the nature of what settlement terms are acceptable. Demands must always be far greater than that which will ultimately be accepted in order to maintain the hard strategy.[2]

The above considerations lie at the heart of the problem of low credibility of negotiators' statements. Tactical considerations require that the parties lie, so observers and interpreters are forced to examine actions rather than words. The negotiators' arguments are ignored in favor of speculation about the significance of the length of coffee breaks.

The above analysis of the tactical choices of negotiators is, of course, too static. In practice strategies are not hard or soft, but harder or softer. Statements are not always completely untrue, for some exchange of reliable information is necessary for the mere maintenance of negotiations, let alone minimal progress toward a solution. Minimum dispositions are subject to change. But tactical pressures of negotiation do create forces pressing toward firmness and distortion. These are countered only by the costs of continuing without a settlement.

For much of the American public, negotiation as an important public decision-making system is most often linked with labor-management bargaining. Last-minute strike-avoiding agreements are frequently newsworthy, and negotiated settlements which end walkouts rate headlines, even on the sports page. Labor negotiations generally succeed in reaching agreements. Compared to contract negotiations which succeed without strikes, those in which strikes are called are few, and most strikes are brief. Although many citizens may find strikes wasteful, they do get settled by negotiation in a relatively short time. To Americans negotiation is a decision-making system which operates under certain rules of fair play and which, while it may bring some inflationary pressures, usually works reasonably well. When we are told that negotiations offer a way to end the Vietnam war, we are likely to think of negotiations in terms of our most frequent experience, collective bargaining.

International negotiation, however, differs in at least four fundamental ways from collective bargaining.

---

[1] For a more thorough discussion of the hard and soft positions see Richard B. Walton and Robert B. McKersie, "Bargaining Dilemmas in Mixed-Motive Decision Making," *Behavioral Science*, vol. 11, #5 (December 1966).

[2] For a more thorough discussion of the minimum disposition problem see David H. Smith, "Communication and Negotiation," in *Communication Spectrum*, ed. Lee Thayer, Milwaukee: NSSC, 1968.

First of all, collective bargaining operates under a contract expiration deadline with the governmental requirement that the parties bargain in good faith. Neither a deadline nor the requirement for good faith bargaining exists in Paris. A deadline changes the tactical mix. The deadline marks the time when costs increase. As a deadline approaches, negotiators become more willing to reveal information and less willing to risk the failure to settle. Last-minute labor agreements are so common that they are no longer surprising, but rather expected. International negotiations, by contrast, do not have a fixed deadline which coerces the parties to bargain. Increased costs for not settling are not associated with a particular point in time. Consequently, international negotiations are much more likely to be protracted than are negotiations under the system most familiar in the United States.

A second difference between collective bargaining and diplomacy is that the strike is a specific, virtually inevitable, mutually punishing consequence of not agreeing. The strike is a highly credible threat. There is little doubt that it will occur at a certain time, that it will bring dramatically increased costs to both sides, and that it can be avoided only by the softening of strategy and decreasing of deception. No similar threat exists in the Paris talks. No threat is built into the system. If, for example, the United States threatens to use nuclear weapons in North Vietnam, the North Vietnamese are not likely to believe that the threat is sincere, and their anticipated disbelief renders an attempt to use such a threat useless as a lever to soften the North Vietnamese tactics. All such threats are arbitrary and depend on specific acts by the parties rather than on the normal functioning of the system. Furthermore, world opinion constrains deliberate acts to punish the other party, and such acts are likely to provide him with an attractive propaganda opportunity which necessitates his withdrawal from the bargaining table. Finally, the strike harms both parties and, consequently, provides pressure on both, whereas a unilateral act punishes only one side and, as such, is seen as part of a hard strategy by one party rather than a pressure for softening by both.

The third difference between the talks in Paris and labor negotiation is that in collective bargaining there is a convention of reciprocal concessions. Both parties assume an exchange of concessions, and opening positions clearly contain demands included for trading purposes only.[3] The opening high demands are viewed by Americans only as a prelude to a scaling down through concessions to a set of mutually acceptable terms. Communist negotiators, on the other hand, do not generally follow the concession trading convention. As in Korea, they tend to offer a position and argue it firmly for a long time. Concessions by their opponents do not bring reciprocal concessions. As a result, systematic progress toward agreement is not apparent to observers, but rather the Communists appear not to be bargaining in good faith.

The fourth important difference between labor relations and international relations is that labor relations require a much closer working relationship between the parties after the agreement. The contract must be administered

---

[3] Interesting in this regard is the National Labor Relations Board's ruling that the "final offer first" strategy of "Boulwarism" used by General Electric which eschewed the trading of concession, was a failure to bargain in good faith and hence an unfair labor practice.

day by day and a new contract negotiated periodically. This continuing relationship constrains the parties from bargaining behavior which will destroy that relationship. But North Vietnam and the United States will not have the same kind of day-to-day relationship; consequently the constraints against invective and bad faith bargaining are much less. Concern for the continuing relationship does not soften international bargaining strategy.

While many Americans think of negotiations as a reliable and not conspicuously inefficient decision system, on an international level, as in Paris, the forces which counter the tendencies to hard strategy and deception are much weaker than they are in the familiar model of collective bargaining.

Although the talks in Paris differ from the familiar model of collective bargaining, American war critics have proposed negotiation as the means to end our involvement in Vietnam. The rhetoric of Vietnam war critics in the United States began before the 1964 Tonkin Gulf Resolution, but it widened its appeal to increasing numbers of politically moderate Americans following Eugene McCarthy's entry into the presidential campaign. McCarthy's showing in the Minnesota precinct caucuses and the New Hampshire primary brought Robert Kennedy into the presidential race and, ultimately, forced Lyndon Johnson out. The arguments which produced these changes were clearly problem centered. Vietnam, it was argued, costs too much in lives and dollars, diverts the attention of the nation from critical problems here at home, divides the generations and races, sacrifices the nation's moral leadership and world position, gives the military undue influence in American life, sets a tone of violence through television coverage of the war, puts the United States on the side of exploitative governments and against the popular will in underdeveloped countries, and robs us of the ability to respond flexibly to problems in other parts of the world. When advocates, whether on the public platform or in the suburban living room, were pressed for a solution to the Vietnam problem few mentioned unilateral withdrawal. Most talked about letting the South Vietnamese do more of the fighting but finally settled the issue by invoking the prospect of a negotiated settlement. Some proposed settlements they would find desirable, but these were to be obtained, of course, at the bargaining table.

At this writing the peace movement has failed to nominate a major party candidate for the presidency, and the Paris talks continue without any indication of substantial progress in the near future. Many doves may find partial satisfaction in Lyndon Johnson's absence from the presidential race, in the anti-war sentiment revealed in the polls and primaries, and in the substantial peace vote on the Democratic platform report in Chicago. But anti-war rhetoric cannot be judged a major success on the basis of its impact on the national political scene. The new politics may have eliminated the unit rule in Texas, but it has not given the American people a presidential choice which promises a real change in Vietnam.

The larger goal was, of course, not just political victory, but peace. Has the rhetoric of doves been any more successful in achieving an end to the fighting in Southeast Asia? The pressure of the peace movement unquestionably influenced Lyndon Johnson's successful effort to begin talks last spring. But have the persuasive efforts of the anti-war speakers made a negotiated settlement more likely? To answer this question we must look not at the American public as the primary audience, but at the North Vietnamese. If one objective of the peace movement was to enable the United States to end its Vietnamese involvement through a negotiated settlement and if the movement had failed to nominate a potentially dovish administration as a means to that goal, then one could speculate on the direct effect of the anti-war rhetoric on the Paris negotiations themselves.

If the North Vietnamese face the two tactical questions mentioned earlier, how hard a negotiating stance to maintain and how much to reveal about the terms they are really willing to accept, then anti-war rhetoric in the United States may have decreased rather than increased the likelihood of a negotiated settlement. The doves focused on the problems Vietnam created for the United States and offered negotiation as a solution clearly with more hope than realism. International bargaining does not have the same built in forces toward quick solution as the more familiar collective bargaining system. Rather, the pressure for softening strategies comes from the costs of continuing without a settlement. How have these pressures been affected by the peace movement?

Ground action doesn't take place in North Vietnam, only part of the fighting is done by North Vietnamese, and weapons and supplies come from Russia and China. It is difficult to assess the war's impact on North Vietnam, but she has apparently found herself able to sustain the costs involved in her single international commitment. The limitation on American bombing that came with President Johnson's peace move last spring reduced those costs. A complete elimination of bombing in the North as advocated in the peace plank debated at the Democratic convention would reduce them further. Just how much bombing hurts North Vietnam we don't know, but a reduction in the cost of not settling can hardly be regarded as a pressure likely to soften North Vietnamese bargaining strategy.

In deciding how hard or soft a strategy to invoke, the wise negotiator anticipates the likely posture of his opponent. If his opponent appears likely to soften his position, the best strategy is to remain firm rather than to soften in return. What influence can widespread support for positions softer than Mr. Harriman's have? Clearly when no deadline makes time pressure important and when costs of not settling are not being increased, the possibility of further United States softening is worth waiting for. If Lyndon Johnson has responded once to dove pressure by limiting bombing, isn't it probable that he will respond again? And as more and more Americans become persuaded by anti-war problem-centered arguments, such a line of reasoning must become more and more persuasive to the North Vietnamese. Brock and Scott argued that North Vietnam would not bargain seriously until a new administration is in office. They apparently mean by serious bargaining the softening of the North Vietnamese bargaining position. But if there were any prospect that the new administration would be headed by a peace candidate with a promise to keep to end the war, North Vietnam might need to soften little at all. Such a prospect would be doubly worth waiting for, particularly if the costs of not settling are not unbearable and increasing.

Thus in regard to the Paris negotiations, the impact of the anti-war rhetoric in the U. S. is ironic. The more successful that rhetoric is in persuading Americans that the war should not continue, the more difficult becomes the task of securing the compromise solution from the North Vietnamese that the doves want so badly.

The term "negotiated settlement" is, of course, ambiguous. The fact that George Wallace, Richard Nixon, Hubert Humphrey, and Eugene McCarthy all favor a negotiated settlement demonstrates that the term is high on the abstraction ladder. If the doves do not mean some compromise which achieves at least some of the United States' policy goals, but rather a virtual unilateral withdrawal, then the result of their success is not as likely to be ironic. If Americans become increasingly eager to get out of Vietnam and if as a result North Vietnam continues to be unyielding, then perhaps the nation will become more willing to accept a unilateral withdrawal and the administration will also become willing to settle for simply pulling out. Some doves undoubtedly mean unilateral withdrawal when they say negotiated settlement, but it takes a cynical analysis indeed to read this intention into the actions of the majority of an idealisic group so dedicated to "telling it like it is." Even those who have favored unilateral withdrawal all along may find their hopes frustrated if, having had its expectation of negotiated settlement aroused and then finding it unfulfilled, the American public turns to the extreme hawks for a quick military end to the war. Here again the irony of rhetorical success at home breeding the ultimate defeat of the foreign policy objective presents itself.

With the nominations of Nixon and Humphrey the possibility of a substantial softening of the United States bargaining strategy seems unlikely. Indeed the prospects for a Nixon victory and/or a strong Wallace showing could lead the North Vietnamese to want to settle with Lyndon Johnson, particularly if they believe what he says about eschewing another term to work for peace.

The nature of international negotiations has created a situation in which the success of the peace movement in persuading the American people that we should negotiate our way out of Vietnam makes the achievement of that end more difficult, while the failure of that persuasion to nominate a peace candidate makes a negotiated settlement more likely. To those of us who have worked for McCarthy, Kennedy, Rockefeller, or other "peace" candidates this irony adds to our already heavy burden of political frustration. The prospect that a potential Nixon victory creates the most favorable conditions for a Vietnamese settlement is almost too much to bear.

ROBERT KENNEDY: A STUDY OF IMAGE CHANGE

James W. Pratt

Immediately after his assassination, *Time* magazine featured Robert Kennedy as its cover subject for the eighth time. The story highlights Kennedy's musing "on all the things he wanted to do and all that he felt he could do: reconcile the races, summon the 'good that's in America,' end the war, get the best and most creative minds into government, broaden the basic idea of the Peace Corps so that people in all walks of life would try to help one another." The writer concludes, "He was ambitious, but not for himself."[1] Less than a month earlier, because of his entry into the contest for the Democratic Presidential nomination, Kennedy had been featured by *Time*. The article relates, "The timing of his entry into the race was proof to many that Kennedy had been slyly scheming all along. . . . His argument that an earlier challenge would have been interpreted as merely anti-L.B.J. animus did not save him from being colored ruthless and opportunistic once again."[2]

The differing evaluations represented in these two quotations—which both refer to Kennedy's entering the Presidential race, appeared in the same magazine, and were written less than a month apart—are typical of the radical change in image which followed Robert Kennedy's assassination and which was expressed by many different journalists. Prior to his assassination, a gradual image change had been taking place. This evolution of Robert Kennedy's public image illustrates a characteristic time lag in the formation of new public images. How, then, is it possible for a striking image reversal such as the one described above to take place within a few weeks?

Kenneth Boulding in his book *The Image* provides a useful framework for examining Kennedy's image. Boulding offers a detailed description of the concept of the public image, which he terms "the basic bond of any society."[3] Although any particular image is the product of an individual mind, Boulding argues that "an enormous part of the activity of each society is concerned with the transmission and protection of its public image; that set of images . . . which is shared by the mass of its people."[4] Important to Boulding's concept of public image is the "transcript" which such an image produces in the form of a relatively permanent record which preserves and publicizes the shared image. Boulding also emphasizes the role which the mass media play in circulating or creating the image of public figures.[5] With this understanding of public images in mind, it might be possible to shed light on the image reversal by examining periods during Robert Kennedy's career when his image "transcript" revealed this time lag in the formation of his public image.

Mr. Pratt is a graduate student and teaching associate in the Department of Speech, Communication, and Theatre Arts at the University of Minnesota.

[1] "Politics and Assassination," *Time*, June 14, 1968, p. 19.

[2] "The Politics of Restoration," *Time*, May 24, 1968, p. 24.

[3] Kenneth Boulding, *The Image* (Ann Arbor: University of Michigan Press, 1956), p. 64. For a further development of Boulding's concept of the public image, see his chapter V, "The Public Image and the Sociology of Knowledge." Theodore Clevenger, Jr., in his book *Audience Analysis* (Indianapolis: The Bobbs-Merrill Co., Inc., 1966) presents a compatible description of images in Chapter 5, "Images in the auditor."

[4] *Ibid.*, p. 64.

[5] *Ibid.*, p. 65.

1

Early in his public career, Kennedy's image was almost wholly a personal one. An examination of the "transcript" of his image as represented by periodical articles during the period prior to 1960 reveals virtually no political comments and a heavy emphasis upon personality description. It is not difficult to understand why this might have been the case. Kennedy's official occupation as legal counsel to Congressional committees during those early years of his career was one which cast him as a representative of other men. Warren Weaver, Jr., called Kennedy the "voice" of Senators Joseph McCarthy and John McClellan and concluded, "To the limited public that was aware of him at all, he was a very young and impersonal legal questioning machine."[6] Kennedy did not—and could not—develop an independent political image during those years. He made no speeches which were available to the general public; and the substantive positions which he supported were always those of the committees which he represented. These early associations were to shape Kennedy's image far into the future. Kennedy biographer William V. Shannon describes those actions which were to associate the images of Kennedy and McCarthy:

> When the Junior Chamber of Commerce chose Kennedy as one of the nation's "Ten Outstanding Young Men," he stayed out of the banquet hall during the main address by Edward R. Murrow because the speech was critical of McCarthy. In McCarthy's last months, when he continued to drink despite a serious liver ailment, Kennedy was one of those who visited him and tried to sustain his morale. At McCarthy's death in 1957, Kennedy not only attended the funeral Mass in Washington but also flew to Appleton, Wisconsin, for the interment.[7]

Several years later, as the chief counsel for John McClellan's Senate Investigating Committee, Kennedy was known for that Committee's exposure of labor union corruption and the prosecution of Teamsters Union presidents Dave Beck and Jimmy Hoffa. Portions of the committee hearings were televised, exposing Kennedy's cross-examination techniques to a national audience. *Time* reported that, as a result of this coverage, "Bobby overshadowed his big brother as a national figure."[8] Although Kennedy was still relatively unknown, his image transcript revealed him as a promising young political conservative.

In 1960, after his brother's election to the Presidency, Robert Kennedy became Attorney General, the first official position in which he was able to establish an independent record. No longer was he the "voice" of other men; and, despite the close public and private relationship which existed between the Kennedy brothers, the Attorney General was not viewed as simply executing the President's wishes.

Kennedy worked quickly to establish a record as an active and liberal Attorney General. Although he readily acknowledged the recency of his interest in civil rights, Kennedy did not allow this to hinder his department's actions in that area. The Justice Department record reveals the accomplishments, particularly in the attempt to gain increased voting rights for Negroes: the number of cases involving Negro voting rights quadrupled in two years,

---

[6] Warren Weaver, Jr., "Will the Real Robert Kennedy Stand Up?" *New York Times Magazine*, June 20, 1965, p. 8.

[7] William V. Shannon, *The Heir Apparent* (New York: Macmillan, 1967), p. 57.

[8] "Little Brother is Watching," *Time*, October 10, 1960, p. 26.

and twenty-three voting rights lawsuits were introduced in the deep South.[9] Kennedy also sent U.S. marshals and deputies into the South to protect "freedom riders" and to control rioting following federally-ordered school integration. He worked with the Interstate Commerce Commission to insure the integration of transportation facilities. Kennedy was instrumental in drafting the civil-rights bill in 1963 which included fair employment and public accommodations provisions. And he argued his first case before any court when he appeared before the U.S. Supreme Court to seek an end to Georgia's "county unit" voting system because it was contrary to the "one person, one vote" principle.[10]

Kennedy's actions during his term as Attorney General, particularly those connected with civil rights, are ones which clearly represent a liberal political position. His speaking, too, reveals a liberal orientation. There is a critical basis for assuming that a speaker will reveal his political orientation in his speaking. Richard Weaver has argued that the sources of argument used by a speaker relate to his political position and that the liberal argues from circumstance whereas the conservative argues from definition.[11] Bernard Brock has developed a set of operational definitions of political positions, based upon the rhetorical strategies employed by the speaker. Among his conclusions are that the liberal seeks to speed the pace of societal change within the existing structure of society and that he characteristically argues from scene (similar to Weaver's "circumstance"); the conservative seeks to slow societal change while emphasizing the role of agent.[12] Kennedy's political speaking while he was Attorney General, when viewed from the perspective of these definitions, reveals a clearly liberal point of view.

Speaking at the University of Georgia on May 6, 1961, Kennedy gave his first formal speech as Attorney General—and one of the earliest public speeches of his career.[13] Perhaps the most salient aspect of the United States civil rights movement at that time was the integration of public schools; Martin Luther King had not yet led his March on Washington, and the destructive summer riots were still in the future. Working within this societal context, it is possible to assess Kennedy's liberal rhetorical strategies in this speech.

Kennedy's scenic, or situational, emphasis emerges early in this speech when he points to the importance of analyzing "the events of the last few weeks" as a basis for governmental action. He is conscious of the role of the United States in the world scene when he points out that "50 per cent of the countries in the United Nations are not white" and comments upon their importance to the United States. Kennedy stresses the importance of understanding and working within the context of Southern society in implementing federal law. Throughout the speech he makes clear his attitude toward change, one which emphasizes accelerating existing programs. Kennedy refers to the necessity of "moving forward" and stresses particularly the

---

[9] "What Makes Bobby Run?" *Newsweek*, March 18, 1963, p. 30.

[10] "The Bobby Kennedy Record," *U. S. News and World Report*, May 6, 1968, p. 52.

[11] Richard Weaver, *The Ethics of Rhetoric* (Chicago: Henry Regnery Co., 1965), pp. 112–113.

[12] Bernard L. Brock, "A Definition of Four Political Positions and a Description of their Rhetorical Characteristics" (unpublished Ph.D. dissertation, Northwestern University, 1965), pp. 40–50, 333–354.

[13] U. S., *Congressional Record*, 87th Cong., 1st Sess., 1961, CVII, Part 6, 7753–7755.

need to "make progress" or "take action." The entire speech is cast within the framework of the rule of law which provides Kennedy with the means for indicating the importance of achieving change within the structure of society. The changes which he advocates are all to take place through the legal process, with an attempt to change and expand law but not to reject it.

The rhetorical techniques which Kennedy uses in this speech identify his political viewpoint as being a liberal one. He indicates his respect for the structure of the legal system, but he advocates more rapid change within this structure. And the basic emphasis of his speech is upon scenic considerations, both in terms of a description of the problems involved in civil rights and the solution required.

Later in his career as Attorney General, on August 12, 1962, Kennedy gave another major speech which also reflects his liberal political orientation.[14] Even the title of the speech—"Much Has Been Accomplished—Much Remains to be Done"—suggests a liberal attitude toward change, which is reiterated a number of times throughout the speech. Kennedy continually refers to achievements made and the need for greater accomplishments. Developing detailed examples, Kennedy points to the specific number of Negroes working in federal agencies and the improvement which this situation represents. A central point of focus in this speech is Kennedy's emphasis upon the beneficial situation which the guarantee of voting rights will create. He says, "We have taken a tremendous amount of action in the field of voting, because it has been our feeling that once you gain the franchise, once an individual is allowed to register and to vote, many of these other rights that we are making an effort to secure for minority groups will come." The emphasis continues through the speech; and, although it is apparent that Kennedy views the achievement of voting rights as a primary aim by itself, he clearly regards their most important function as being the establishment of a favorable situation within which other rights may be gained. This view toward the acquisition of voting rights is also consistent with a liberal attitude toward change: working within the structure of the legal system, Kennedy encourages more rapid change. In this same vein, he comments on federal integration accomplishments in education by saying that "we have a great deal more to do and certainly the job is not done."

The liberal rhetorical characteristics are clearly present in this speech. Always accepting the legal structure of society, Kennedy advocates more rapid change and the need for greater accomplishments. The discussion of civil rights which he offers concentrates heavily upon the importance of situational factors in making the gains which he encourages.

On the basis of these observations, one can conclude that Kennedy represented a consistently liberal position, in his actions and in his speeches, during his term as Attorney General. An examination of the "transcript" of Kennedy's public image during that period, however, reveals a marked preference for characterizing Kennedy as being a conservative.

Typical of the judgments of Kennedy's political position is this observation by Robert Manning: "His reflexes are by background conservative and, a close friend says, 'Liberal' is still apt to be a dirty word to Bobby."[15] Dan Wakefield expresses the confusion regarding Kennedy's political position—and the reluctance to accept perceived change—when he writes, "The term

---

[14] U.S., *Congressional Record*, 87th Cong., 2nd Sess., 1962, CVIII, Part 12, 16805–16806.

[15] Robert Manning, "Someone the President Can Talk To," *New York Times Magazine*, May 28, 1961, p. 29.

'liberal' is usually uttered with an inflection of irony by Bob Kennedy, yet many of his political convictions would have to be described by that label. It no more adequately describes his outlook, however, than the word 'conservative.'"[16] Gore Vidal evaluates Kennedy as being basically conservative when he writes, "It is apparent that Bobby's view of men and actions is a good deal closer to that of Barry Goldwater's than it is to that of his brother."[17] Although several writers tentatively suggest Kennedy's liberal outlook during this period, none seems willing to categorize him as being a liberal without significant qualification. The position revealed in Kennedy's actions and speeches during this period does not appear to justify such reservations.

By the time Kennedy entered the Senate, in 1965, much of this journalistic reserve had disappeared. Writers seemed to be more willing to categorize Kennedy as a liberal, although several express surprise at what they regard as a recent change: William V. Shannon wrote as recently as 1966 that those who had seen Kennedy as a conservative "are now doing an about-face."[18] *U.S. News and World Report* expressed similar reservations, reporting that "Robert Kennedy is suspected of having latent 'conservative' tendencies" despite the fact that "the ADA now credits him with a 94 per cent 'liberal' voting record."[19] A very frequent judgment was that Kennedy had moved "slightly to the left of center." Even more reservation had been expressed before Kennedy's election to the Senate, when *Time* reported that New York's reform Democrats considered Kennedy "much too conservative for their liking."[20]

2

What might account for this failure of Kennedy's public image to reflect his actual political position? Few aspects of the empirical record of Kennedy's actions and speeches during this period can be found to justify a conservative political image. Perhaps best remembered is Kennedy's persistent prosecution of union leader Jimmy Hoffa (although the consensus of legal opinion seems to be that Kennedy did not abuse Hoffa's civil liberties); less known, but still publicly discussed, is Kennedy's advocation of government-authorized wiretapping. Yet these instances seem to be quite overshadowed by Kennedy's liberal civil rights record as Attorney General and his consistently liberal voting record while in the Senate: he scored a 100 per cent liberal record during his last two years in Congress, as judged by the Americans for Democratic Action, and the AFL-CIO rated his record 100 per cent pro-union during his first three years in Congress.[21]

The key to this image lag seems to lie primarily in the record of Kennedy's early associations. Joseph McCarthy's negative image was highly salient to the American people; and his political position was conservative to reactionary. That Kennedy was associated with such a highly public conservative figure—and that he maintained this association with overtly public acts,

[16] Dan Wakefield, "Bobby," *Esquire*, April, 1962, p. 126.

[17] Gore Vidal, "The Best Man: 1968," *Esquire*, March, 1963, p. 60.

[18] William V. Shannon, "Bob Kennedy's Future," *Commonweal*, March 18, 1966, p. 686.

[19] "Kennedy vs. Humphrey: What It's All About," *U.S. News and World Report*, March 28, 1966, p. 55.

[20] "Carpetbagger," *Time*, August 21, 1964, p. 18.

[21] Robert Yoakum, "Kennedy and McCarthy: A Look at Some Votes," *New Republic*, May 11, 1968, p. 23, and "The Bobby Kennedy Record," p. 53.

in spite of McCarthy's general disfavor—identified his political position with that of McCarthy. There were no independent public actions to counteract this impression for several years; and Kennedy's highly publicized cross-examination of union leaders during his term as chief legal counsel for the McClellan committee did nothing to change this established public image. When Kennedy began to develop his own record of actions and statements in regard to political issues in the office of Attorney General, his conservative image by association had already been built and was firmly established in the public mind. Kennedy's associations were all the raw material on which the "transcript" could be grounded. As a result, his record of liberal actions and statements appeared to be new—and the "change" was regarded with skepticism.

The observations presented here are not intended to negate the validity of Kennedy's public image as a reflection of his actual record. Rather, they reveal some important characteristics of his public image. The development of Kennedy's image demonstrates the significance of early images in influencing the later development of the image. Important, too, is the effect in shaping later images which resulted from the association between Kennedy, whose public image was latent and undeveloped, with Joseph McCarthy, whose public image was salient and clear. Great difficulty and little success surrounded Kennedy's extensive and repeated attempts to change that already well developed image, despite the somewhat tenuous basis for its initial formation. Kennedy's image development also reveals an apparently inevitable time lag which follows a change in a person's record of actions and statements and precedes a change in that person's public image. The assassination, a sudden and dramatic terminal event, rapidly accelerated an image change already underway. The traditional ethic of refraining from criticizing the recently dead dictated a concentration upon the favorable aspects of Kennedy's image; and the immediacy of the event required a consultation with those most recently associated with him for formation of the image. At death, Kennedy's image was changed rapidly because it was instantly updated.

Few would deny that John Kennedy's assassination had a profound effect upon the public image of his younger brother Robert, and Robert Kennedy's assassination has already significantly altered the public image of his younger brother Edward—so much so that many feel that the last of the Kennedy brothers could have won the Democratic Presidential nomination simply by appearing at the Democratic convention. To assert that the Kennedy assassinations alone have changed Edward Kennedy's image to that of potential President would be overstatement; but it is apparent that Robert Kennedy's assassination has had an impact on the formation of more images than his own.

THE RHETORIC OF POLITICAL REVOLT:
GEORGE C. WALLACE

David L. Swanson

Nineteen hundred sixty-eight will be remembered as a year of upheaval unprecedented in the recent history of American politics. Controversial leaders were assassinated. Obedience to the rule of law became more and more selective. Important divisions appeared between young and old, between rich and poor, between black and white. Even the venerable two-party system, its sanctity no longer inviolate in this cataclysmic year, was shaken by talk of multiple parties.

The man doing most of the shaking was George Corley Wallace, former Governor of Alabama. A sort of ideological "yard child" of Huey P. Long, Wallace created what has been called the most significant third-party movement in American politics since Theodore Roosevelt's Bull Moose campaign of 1912. In this period of the alienated and the disaffected in American politics, Wallace may be a man well suited to the times. At the age of forty-seven he is entering the second decade of his revolt against the political leadership of our nation. This paper examines the nature of that revolt and focuses on the key rhetorical strategies of Wallace's 1968 Presidential campaign.

I

From his early days in Alabama politics Wallace has decried what he sees as an alarming and rapidly increasing concentration of unconstitutional power in branches of the federal government. In a speech delivered at the University of Missouri-Kansas City in October of 1967, he gave this general tendency specific application:

> We're talking about the elite cult that has grown up in our country of pseudo-intellectuals who today do not think that the average man-on-the-street can get up in the morning or go to bed at night unless this pseudo-intellectual in all of his brilliance writes him the guideline and writes him the blueprint. But the average man-on-the-street . . . he doesn't need guidelines to tell him how to run his business. Nor does he need guidelines to tell him how to run his domestic democratic institutions.[1]

George Wallace's ultimate goal, then, is to institute a system of government which he has called by many names—constitutional government, states' rights, territorial democracy, dual sovereignty. But whatever name it bears, the Wallace "philosophy of government" is characterized by its insistence that state and local governments be ensured the right to regulate their own "domestic democratic institutions," and that in this manner government be "returned to the people."

The present form of the Wallace movement—full-blown Presidential candidacy—is no ill-considered venture. Rather, it represents the fourth phase in a continuing crusade for George Wallace and his style of government. The first phase of Wallace's program sought to challenge "unconsti-

This is a revised version of a paper Mr. Swanson, a Graduate School Honors Fellow in Speech Communication at the University of Kansas, presented in Chicago at the 1968 Central States Speech Association Convention.

[1] George C. Wallace, address delivered at the University of Missouri-Kansas City, Kansas City, Missouri, October 6, 1967.

tutional" federal actions in the courts. As an Alabama circuit judge in 1958, Wallace purposely withheld voter registration records from investigators of the newly-created Civil Rights Commission. In June, 1963, he made his famous stand in the "schoolhouse door" of the University of Alabama. Both of these incidents resulted in Wallace's citation for contempt of a federal court order, but circumstances were such that the constitutional challenge to federal authority he sought never materialized.

When litigation thus proved unsatisfactory, the Wallace program entered a second phase with his attempt to provide the leadership necessary to unify the "solid South." He told the Mississippi State Legislature in November, 1962, that the restoration of Southern unity would allow him to exert powerful pressure on the leadership of the two national parties and thereby win valuable concessions.[2] The visceral politics of the South are not "solid," however, and George Wallace could not make them so.

Phase three of the Wallace program began with the Governor's participation in the 1964 Presidential primary elections. He hoped a strong showing there would force the national political parties to "heed his message" of popular discontent. With a surprisingly strong showing in the primaries and the nomination of Senator Goldwater assured, Wallace withdrew his candidacy, noting that he had accomplished his purpose: his message had been sent to the "high councils of both major political parties."[3]

After Goldwater's decisive defeat, the Wallace movement was forced to enter yet another phase in its quest for power. As the Governor told a Birmingham audience in 1966, "If we had stayed in the race, we would have gotten more votes than the National Republican candidate got. . . . So I say if you defeat [the National Democrats] you've got to do it in some other manner."[4] Seeing no chance for "acceptable" candidates or platforms from the major parties, Wallace decided a third party candidacy was the "other manner" best suited to advancing his movement in 1968.

Two aspects of the Wallace campaign are especially significant. First, its following and its appeal have assured it a place of importance in the history of American politics. Representing a rejection of the course the American government has pursued vis-a-vis social issues since the second World War, the campaign mustered nationwide support in numbers sufficient to provoke reevaluation of the national sentiment. At this writing it seems probable that Wallace will appear on the Presidential ballot in all fifty states. Current polls suggest that he may win 20 to 30% of the popular vote and a larger electoral vote than Hubert Humphrey, the Democratic candidate.

Second, the rhetorical aspects of the Wallace campaign provide a fertile field for inquiry. In a time when Presidential candidates are convinced of the wisdom of selecting moderate positions on issues, the Wallace position is extreme. In a time when issues are said to be irrelevant to the voters' choice of a candidate, Wallace speaks to the issues and wins support. Combatting the influence of party affiliation and traditional voting habits, the Wallace campaign is intensely rhetorical. Unlike the candidates of established parties, Wallace relies on rhetoric to win supporters to his cause, away from ingrained allegiances.

---

[2] George C. Wallace, address delivered to the Mississippi State Legislature, Jackson, Mississippi, November, 1962.

[3] George C. Wallace, "Face the Nation," C.B.S. telecast, July 19, 1964.

[4] George C. Wallace, address delivered at the Kickoff Rally for Mrs. George C. Wallace, Birmingham, Alabama, September 29, 1966.

II

As the Wallace campaign moved closer to the election of 1968 and a critical juncture in its bid for national power, it faced four imposing barriers to success: (1) Wallace was virtually without political allies or influence outside the South; (2) a Wallace victory in 1968 had an aura of implausibility for the voters; (3) Wallace's racist image alienated voters who would otherwise support him; and (4) Wallace could not hope for support from all sections of the electorate. It is through an analysis of the tactics used in meeting these problems that the nature of the rhetoric of George Wallace's political revolt becomes clear.

When a major party candidate embarks on a national campaign, he can normally count on the support of influential politicians throughout the nation. The Wallace campaign had no such allies; any success it experienced was due to Mr. Wallace and to his organization. Because of this lack of influential backing, the Wallace campaign was forced to place primary reliance on rhetoric as a means of securing support. Bill Jones, Wallace's press agent and campaign manager, writes that Wallace realized he must "jump over the politicians' heads and reach the people."[5] To secure this public exposure Wallace delivered one hundred twenty speeches in a six-week campaign to win his third party a position on the California ballot. He spoke frequently to college audiences even though they were often hostile, because campus appearances provide "an excellent forum for a speaker who wishes to have his message known nation wide."[6] His campaign was engineered to attract maximum press coverage, and much of the campaign's limited budget was channelled into programs aired over the national broadcast media. The Wallace campaign, then, sought to counteract a lack of political support by taking its message "to the people," and it is through the effective use of such rhetoric that the movement attacked its other major problems.

A second problem the campaign faced was the implausibility of a Wallace victory. The reluctance of voters to support a candidate who seems to have no chance of victory is a harsh reality of American politics. To fight this incredulity Wallace employed two broad strategies. In the plea for support which constituted the peroration of a typical campaign speech, Wallace pointed out that in a three-way race only thirty-four percent of the vote is needed to give a candidate victory and that he received this much and more in the primaries of 1964. To the critics who called Wallace a "spoiler" who sought only to throw the election into the House of Representatives, he replied that his goal was outright victory and depicted broad support for his campaign among "the people" who had become alienated from the major political parties:

> I am in this race because I believe the American people have been pushed around long enough, and that they, like you and I, are fed up with the continuous trend toward a socialist state which now subjects the individual to the dictates of an all-powerful central government.[7]

A third, more important problem facing Wallace was his image as a radical and a racist. Early in 1968 political opinion pollster Louis Harris

---

[5] Bill Jones, *The Wallace Story* (Northport, Alabama: American Southern Publishing Company, 1966), p. 71.

[6] *Ibid.*, p. 105.

[7] George C. Wallace, address delivered in Atlanta, Georgia, July 4, 1962.

called this image the "great limiting factor," observing that a much larger number of Americans agreed with Wallace on important issues than the polls indicate, but that they were frightened away from supporting him because of his image as a radical.[8] In place of the racist label the Wallace campaign tried to substitute a new image in which its candidate was merely an idealist crusading for a philosophy of government. The radical image, it was contended, was the product of a deliberate distortion of Wallace's position by a hostile national press. As evidence of this new focus, Wallace said on "Meet the Press" last year when asked if he favored segregation:

> I do not recommend segregation in any phase of our society in any state in this Union. I only recommend that the states of the Union continue to determine the policies of their domestic democratic institutions themselves and that the bureaucrats and the theoreticians in Washington let people in Ohio and New York and California decide themselves, for instance, what type of school system they are going to have. I recommend states' rights and local government, and territorial democracy is what I recommend.[9]

In reply to allegations that his support came from a "white backlash," Wallace contended it was due merely to "an ever-growing tendency on the part of the American people to be fed up with big government."[10] Practical implementation of this attempt at image building was seen in Wallace's campaign speeches, each of which contained a recitation of the Negro majority his wife received in her 1966 gubernatorial race. Wallace felt, therefore, that the negative set of the voting public with regard to his racism had to be broken before any effective persuasion could take place.

How successful was this campaign to change the Wallace image? Robert Pearman wrote in his analysis of the Wallace movement:

> When Wallace gets through explaining, somehow he has erased the image of Governor Wallace symbolically blocking the door of the University of Alabama against the admittance of Negro students, or of his battle against federal voter registration in the South. Instead there has emerged the image of George Wallace the oppressed, assaulted by "bearded professors" and maddened throngs of students at Dartmouth, badgered and harrassed by representatives of the federal government, criticized, hounded, and lied about by the nation's press and national television.[11]

A final problem Wallace encountered was the virtual impossibility of his winning the support of certain sectors of the populace: the liberals and perhaps even the moderates, the intellectuals, the upper- and upper-middle-class groups, the Negroes. While Presidential campaigns typically attempt to draw support from every important stratum of the electorate, George Wallace realized that his campaign, to be successful, had to deviate from that pattern. Mr. Wallace, therefore, "wrote off" these groups and focused instead on that segment of the voting public whose support he believed he could win—white voters in the lower- and lower-middle-income groups.

He saw this public as discontented over a number of policies of the federal

---

[8] James K. Batten, "Wallace May Upset Apple Carts," *Kansas City Star*, January 11, 1968, p. 29.

[9] George C. Wallace, "Meet the Press," N.B.C. telecast, April 23, 1967.

[10] *Ibid.*

[11] Robert Pearman, "Wallace Sees Himself as Man of Destiny," *Kansas City Star*, November 19, 1967, Sec. A., p. 21.

government. His task, then, was to arouse this latent discontent and demonstrate how it fit into his broad "philosophy of government." Wallace used three strategies to accomplish this purpose.

First, he identified with them. The theme of his campaign was, "Can a former truck driver who is married to a former dime-store clerk and whose father was a plain dirt farmer be elected President of the United States?"[12] Wallace's speeches evidenced a quest for communion with all the downtrodden "little people" whom the federal government had betrayed and who, through him, could regain control of their destiny. Pearman observed:

> When the crowd is right, George Wallace is a little man carrying the little man's burden. You can hear the up-to-date version of Robert Penn Warren's "Willie Stark," a rustic demagogue of *All the King's Men.*[13]

Second, Wallace attempted to unite his audience of "little people" against their common foes, the pseudo-intellectuals who held power in the federal government. The typical Wallace campaign speech used the term "pseudo-intellectuals" at least twenty times, referring to those people who, "learned but without wisdom," had imperiled the future of the nation. In his Inaugural Address, Governor Wallace pleaded, "let us assume the leadership of the fight and carry our leadership across this nation. God has placed us here in this crisis. Let us not fail in this, our most historic moment."[14] The appeal for unity in the face of the enemy was repeated in his Long Beach, California, address of November, 1967:

> And to those who say I hate to change from the Democratic party or the Republican party, well let me say that the only thing that is going to help save our country is boldness and imagination. And if you've got boldness and imagination enough to make it possible to say to the two parties we're going to have a choice, then you join the American Independent Party and that's going to have a terrific impact.[15]

Wallace's third strategy in eliciting the support of the "common people" was to invest in them a sense of the strength they could wield and to secure their dedication to the solemn task before them. His speeches were replete with references to his support in every section of the country. The impression was created that it was Wallace, not the major political parties, who had the support of "the people." The strength that derives from their numbers must be used, Wallace insisted, to fulfill their sacred duty. Their philosophy of government was "destined to be a national philosophy—embraced by millions of Americans—which shall assume the mantle of leadership and steady a governmental structure in these days of crisis."[16] Wallace completed the task by conveying to his audience a sense of confidence in their eventual victory:

> I am going to take our fight to the people—the court of public opinion—where truth and common sense will eventually prevail.[17]

---

[12] "A New Look at Wallace—What He May Do to the Election," *U.S. News & World Report,* January 29, 1968, p. 57.

[13] Pearman, *loc. cit.*

[14] Jones, *op. cit.*, p. 77.

[15] George C. Wallace, address delivered in Long Beach, California, November 26, 1967.

[16] George C. Wallace, address delivered in Atlanta, Georgia, July 4, 1962.

[17] *Ibid.*

III

This, in brief, was the rhetoric of George Wallace's political revolt. It isolated its target audience, carried its message directly to them, unified them into a solid force with Wallace at its head, and imposed upon them a solemn mission.

Although at this writing the election is still one month away, it has become apparent that George Wallace succeeded in attracting support throughout the nation. Why was this extremist, sectional candidate so successful? Pearman's observation that "He knows the subtleties, the pressure points so to speak, of a certain segment of the American people" provides a fair operational definition of effective rhetoric.[18] For a sizable proportion of the American electorate, George Wallace's appeal was attractive and the rhetorical strategies of his campaign were sound.

While there are many critics who would prefer to practice their art on more palatable oratory, all must agree that George Corley Wallace was a vital participant in the rhetoric of 1968.

---

[18] Pearman, *loc. cit.*

NONVIOLENCE AND BLACK POWER: CIVIL RIGHTS AS A MASS MOVEMENT

JAMES F. KLUMPP

The concept of Black Power changed the focus of the Civil Rights movement from the nonviolent predominantly Southern movement to the aggressive nationwide movement. The developments in Civil Rights during 1968, the death of Dr. Martin Luther King and the relative quiet last summer in the cities, have raised several interesting questions about the two phases of the Civil Rights movement: Where do we go from here? What type of leader can be expected to head the Black Power movement in the future? Will the aggressive militancy increase or will the movement begin to consolidate its power?

In his book *The True Believer* longshoreman-philosopher Eric Hoffer offers a model for mass movements that may suggest answers to these questions. Hoffer's model both helps clarify the past relationship between the nonviolent and the Black Power phases of the movement and provides possible future directions for the Black Power movement.

Hoffer defines mass movement in terms of its essential characteristics: "All mass movements generate in their adherents a readiness to die and a proclivity for united action; all of them, irrespective of the doctrine they preach and the program they project, breed fanaticism, enthusiasm, fervent hope, hatred and intolerance; all of them are capable of releasing a powerful flow of activity in certain departments of life; all of them demand blind faith and singlehearted allegiance."[1]

Central to this view is the complete subordination of the individual to the movement. To be a mass movement in Hoffer's use of the term, the movement must be the end and the means of all its members. When the movement becomes all important, it will breed fanaticism, and reinforce its domination over the individual by cultivating hope, hatred, and intolerance.

This paper compares the rhetorical approaches of Martin Luther King, leader of the nonviolent movement, and Stokely Carmichael, leader (at least in the early stages) of the Black Power movement, and relates the approaches to Hoffer's model. Both speeches examined urge support for the leader's particular methods of social change. King's speech, "Love, Law, and Civil Disobedience," delivered November 16, 1961, to the annual meeting of the Fellowship of the Concerned, explains nonviolence and self-suffering as a method of social protest. Carmichael's speech, "Black Power," delivered in Chicago July 28, 1966, emphasizes the virtues of black unity. The respective rhetorical approaches to individualism, self-sacrifice, and hatred are compared and then possible future directions for Black Power will be suggested based on Hoffer's model.

Mr. Klumpp is a graduate student and teaching associate in the Department of Speech, Communication and Theatre Arts at the University of Minnesota.

[1] Eric Hoffer, *The True Believer* (New York: Harper and Row, 1951), p. 9.

In a mass movement the relationship between the individual and the movement becomes very important. The first and most fundamental difference between the rhetorical positions of Martin Luther King and Stokely Carmichael in their respective speeches lies in the approach of each to the relationship between the individual and the movement.

King suggests that his movement is merely a group of individuals and not a unified mass. Freedom is the keynote of King's movement—freedom for the individual. Perhaps the best definition of the individual freedom that the movement seeks is King's phrase "true person-to-person relationships."[2] The end of the movement is its dissolution; it is formed and operates only to gain individual rights for its individual members.

King contends that the means and ends of a movement must cohere[3] and the emphasis on the individual in the means of the movement certainly is consistent with the emphasis on the individual in the ends of the movement. Civil disobedience is, of course, based on deliberate violation of unjust laws. King's criterion for a just law is whether or not the law "degrades the human personality."[4] Such laws the individual can refuse to obey if he is willing to accept the punishment for his violation. According to King, even the decision of which laws to disobey is the individual's and not the movement's.[5] Once the individual decides to protest, the confrontation that eventually leads to accomplishment of the movement's goals is between the individual who is engaged in the nonviolent struggle and the oppressing forces. The movement is only the collective body of individual actions moving toward the common individual goals.

In sharp contrast, Carmichael's speech is not a battle plan for individual action but for the action of the "black people." The individual is no longer the actor, the actor is the black people as an unit. Carmichael's speech is "about what black people have to do."[6] His suggestion is that "It's time black people got together,"[7] and once they are together they act as an entity. "We" is the subject of Carmichael's imperatives of action. Only twice in the entire speech does he get so individual as to use the second person singular "you" subject. When the white man is spoken to or moved against it is "we," the black people, that do the speaking and moving. Thus the black individual must cease to exist except as a part of the black people. The individual must forfeit his identity to the movement, just as Carmichael forfeits his own identity in this speech. In the speech Carmichael has no voice, rather the movement has Carmichael's voice.

Hoffer says that identification with the movement instead of with the self promotes self-sacrifice so necessary to a mass movement's methods. He writes:

To ripen a person for self-sacrifice he must be stripped of his individual identity and distinctness. He must cease to be George, Hans, Ivan, or Tadao—a human atom with an existence bounded by birth and death.

---

[2] Martin Luther King, "Love, Law, and Civil Disobedience," in *Rhetoric of Racial Revolt*, ed. Roy L. Hill (Denver: Golden Bell Press, 1964), p. 354.

[3] *Ibid.*, p. 347.

[4] *Ibid.*, p. 351.

[5] *Ibid.*, p. 352.

[6] Stokely Carmichael, "Black Power," delivered in Chicago on July 28, 1966, and printed by Chicago SNCC, reprinted in *The Burden of Race*, ed. Gilbert Osofsky (New York: Harper and Row, 1967), p. 630.

[7] *Ibid.*, p. 629.

> The most drastic way to achieve this end is by the complete assimi-
> lation of the individual into a collective body. The fully assimilated
> individual does not see himself and others as human beings. When
> asked who he is, his automatic response is that he is a German, a Russian,
> a Japanese, a Christian, a Moslem, [or a black].[8]

King's movement violates Hoffer's criterion for a mass movement. The individual has to forfeit individual identity and individual judgment, Hoffer
says. King did not require such forfeiture, Carmichael does. For Carmichael
there are only black people and white people. There is no individual
existence outside of this classification.

Hoffer says that the individual must become thoroughly submerged in
the movement in order that self-sacrifice, a necessary result of a mass movement's approach, will be accepted by its members. Both of the Civil Rights
movements require self-sacrifice, but the rhetorical strategies to induce
self-sacrifice provide a second contrast between the two speeches.

King's speech contains a very obvious and well developed strategy for
convincing the audience of the value of self-sacrifice. To King self-sacrifice
is an actual method, the direct stimulus that is to accomplish the goal of
integration. King says, "The non-violent say that suffering becomes a
powerful social force when you willingly accept that violence on yourself
. . . suffering may serve to transform the social situation."[9] Thus since suffering is the direct method of the movement, the strategy of convincing the
Negro to follow this method involves a justification of suffering. Suffering
will be effective, King argues, because eventually people will recognize the
justice of the end and the goodness of the means of the nonviolent movement. Faith in the future, faith that the goals are inevitable, is the reason
the nonviolent are willing to suffer.

Suffering does not play the same role in Carmichael's movement that it
plays in King's movement. While suffering is actually the direct stimulus in
King's movement, in Carmichael's movement suffering is but an inevitable
result of the confrontation that the mass movement uses to disrupt society.
Thus King's strategy is passive, absorbing suffering, while Carmichael's is
active, afflicting suffering.

In the Carmichael speech persuasive strategy urges aggressive confrontation with the white power structure and the black suffering is not mentioned.
He says, "We have to define how we are going to move. . . . We have to
build a strong base to let them know if they touch one black man driving
his wife to the hospital in Los Angeles, or one black man walking down a
highway in Mississippi or if they take one black man who has a rebellion and
put him in jail and start talking treason, we are going to disrupt this whole
country."[10]

Hoffer's model helps explain the different rhetorical approaches to suffering in the two speeches. In King's movement the emphasis on individualism
destroys the ability of the movement itself to induce self-sacrifice without an
overt rhetorical strategy. Hoffer explains the limitations individuality im-
poses on the willingness to suffer: "The unavoidable conclusion seems to be

---

[8] Hoffer, p. 60.
[9] King, pp. 349–350.
[10] Carmichael, p. 631.

that when the individual faces torture or annihilation, he cannot rely on the resources of his own individuality. His only source of strength is in not being himself but part of something mighty, glorious and indestructible. . . . The destiny of one's religion, nation, race, party or family."[11]

King does not have the advantage of such an absolute commitment to the movement. King's first strategy is to construct a cause—in this case justice. The success of the movement is inevitable, King argues, because people will recognize its justice. Justice will triumph over the oppression of the system. This strategy, however, separates the movement from the inevitable cause, so a second strategy is required to persuade the followers to suffer for the movement. King must, therefore, argue overtly for the power of suffering.

Carmichael can use the identification with the movement as the persuasive agency to induce self-sacrifice. The followers gladly sacrifice because they are subordinated to a cause. Therefore, Carmichael is spared the necessity for a direct rhetorical strategy to induce suffering.

If the unification of the individual and the mass movement becomes the key to self-sacrifice, how is unification accomplished? The difference between the positions of King and Carmichael on the ways of unity helps explain the presence of identification with the group in Carmichael's movement and the lack of identification in King's.

King's movement is based on love not hatred, and love is the theme of his speech. The rhetorical strategy used to urge love for all other men and still oppose the human institution of segregation is to create an oppressor as vague as possible. King notes, "one seeks to defeat the unjust system, rather than individuals who are caught in that system."[12] The most specific term that King uses to denote the segregationists is "reactionary forces in the South."[13] It is easier to love one's oppressor if the oppression seems only a tool of some vague unseen force. Thus King can support the personalized "love ethic" while opposing the impersonal segregation system.

Carmichael is, however, preoccupied with hatred in his speech. He creates the white people as his devil. "The white people . . . force us to live the way we live,"[14] he says. The white people are blamed for every wrong. This strategy clearly delineates the opposition to the black people and establishes a devil as a scapegoat for the black's problems.

Hoffer explains hatred as "the most accessible and comprehensive of all unifying agents."[15] It helps separate the individual from himself and join the collective whole in mutual hatred. The object of the hate, the devil, is singular so that hatred can be unified and intense within the movement; is omnipotent and omnipresent so all the failures of the movement may be blamed on the devil and all successes be victories over the devil; and foreign so that it is clearly identified as outside of the movement.

King's movement has only love, no devil and no real hatred, but Carmichael's "white people" fits the model. "White people" form a corporate whole. Carmichael reacts strongly against the whites who supposedly sympathize with the movement. They are foreigners and "nothing but traitorous enemies."[16] The white people are the cause of all Negro problems

---

[11] Hoffer, p. 62.
[12] King, p. 349.
[13] Ibid., p. 345.
[14] Carmichael, p. 632.
[15] Hoffer, p. 85.
[16] Carmichael, p. 631.

and they are foreign because they are not black. "They oppress us because we are black,"[17] Carmichael charges.

Having oriented the Civil Rights movement within Hoffer's mass movement model, perhaps now an answer should be offered to one of the black leaders' favorite recent questions: Where do we go from here? For the rhetorician the question is: What kind of leader and what kind of rhetoric would Hoffer's model predict from the black community?

In successful mass movements Hoffer recognizes three leadership types—the man of words who discredits the prevailing order, the fanatic who institutes the mass movement phase, and the man of action who consolidates the gains of the movement. Martin Luther King had many of the characteristics of Hoffer's man of words. Hoffer explains, "Mass movements do not usually rise until the prevailing order has been discredited. The discrediting is not an automatic result of the blunders and abuses of those in power, but the deliberate work of men of words with a grievance."[18] It was King's efforts in the South that made the Civil Rights problem a salient national issue and discredited the white social structure. The Southern movement under King became a rhetorical device for discrediting the prevailing order.

If King was a man of words, Stokely Carmichael was the fanatic of the Civil Rights movement. Hoffer says of the fanatic:

> When the moment is ripe, only the fanatic can hatch a genuine mass movement. Without him the disaffection engendered by militant men of words remains undirected and can vent itself only in pointless and easily suppressed disorders. Without him the initiated reforms, even when drastic, leave the old way of life unchanged, and any change in government usually amounts to no more than a transfer of power from one set of men of action to another. Without him there can perhaps be no new beginning.[19]

At the present time there is less evidence of a fanatic leader in the Civil Rights movement than at times in the past. Whether Carmichael's demise in the Black Power movement is due to his disconcern for the movement in favor of the Viet Nam cause, or to the Negroes' withdrawal of support from him is unclear. If the former is the explanation Hoffer's model offers an explanation: "Where mass movements are in violent competition with each other, there are not infrequent instances of converts—even the most zealous—shifting their allegiance from one to the other."[20] Carmichael did not really move to a *competing* mass movement but the zealousness with which he has opposed the Viet Nam involvement indicates that he may view the Viet Nam opposition as his new mass movement.

If the Negroes rejected Carmichael, the short-lived nature of the fanatic stage of the movement would suggest that if the movement is a true mass movement another leader will take Carmichael's place. The rhetorician may anticipate reactivation of the movement if Carmichael returns or a new leader of the Carmichael style emerges.

When (and if) the fanatic stage does begin anew, it will have greater intensity than before the present lull. Hoffer notes that self-sacrifice and

[17] *Ibid.*, p. 630.
[18] Hoffer, p. 119.
[19] *Ibid.*, p. 130.
[20] *Ibid.*, p. 25.

unity reinforce each other.[21] Thus the movement intensifies as it feeds upon itself.

When the fanatical or mass movement stage of the movement is complete the man of action enters to consolidate the movement's gains. Hoffer writes: "[The man of action's] appearance usually marks the end of the dynamic phase of the movement. The war with the present is over. The genuine man of action is intent not on renovating the world but on possessing it. Whereas the life breath of the dynamic phase was protest and a desire for drastic change, the final phase is chiefly preoccupied with administering and perpetuating the power won."[22] When the Civil Rights movement completes the fanatical or mass movement stage (it is, of course, very possible that Carmichael's demise indicates that this stage is complete) the rhetorician may expect a man of action who wields the newly won Black Power to overhaul the social structure. Such forces as Julian Bond or the new Negro coalition in Congress should be watched as possible agents of this stage of the mass movement.

Perhaps a paper applying the Hoffer model ought to end as Hoffer ends the preface of *The True Believer*: "The book passes no judgements, and expresses no preferences. It merely tries to explain; and the explanations— all of them theories—are in the nature of suggestions and arguments even when they are stated in what seems a categorical tone."[23]

---

[21] *Ibid.*, p. 59.
[22] *Ibid.*, p. 135.
[23] *Ibid.*, p. 11.

DISPOSITIO IN THE RHETORIC OF A FORMER DEBATER: GEORGE CORLEY WALLACE

L. Dean Fadely*

> The speech is added to, subtracted from and tinkered with from time to time but it does not really change. Only modest amendments of style, indeed, distinguish it from the rhetoric that elected first George, then Lurleen, governor of Alabama.[1]
>
> NEWSWEEK

Throughout the 1968 Presidential campaign, one candidate delivered essentially the same address, in terms of content if not format, at every political rally. There were occasions when it seemed as if he would vary the content of his discourse.[2] However, a mimetic-orator cannot easily change his message, and George Wallace was and is a mimetic-orator.[3] This repetitiveness, however, did not discourage Wallace's supporters. To the contrary, they found in it additional reasons for admiration. To them, Wallace was being honest, forthright, and consistent. Let the other candidates say one thing in one part of the country and another thing in another part of the country. George Wallace would say the same thing in all parts of the country.[4] *The Florence Times and Tri-Cities Daily*, which is published in Florence, Alabama, expressed aspects of this attitude in the following editorial:

> The major news media have criticized George Wallace for making "the same speech" wherever he campaigns.
> Tri-Cities Newspapers believe he has it down pretty good and will laud his continuing to say the same thing.[5]

---

* Mr. Fadely, a Ph.D. candidate in Rhetoric and Public Address at the University of Pittsburgh, is the Director of Forensics at the University of North Carolina at Greensboro. Much of the material included in this paper was gathered during a seminar in Modern Presidential Public Address taught at the University of Pittsburgh by Theodore O. Windt.

[1] "Wallace and His Folks," *Newsweek*, (September 16, 1968), p. 26.

[2] On at least three different occasions different speeches dealing with such diverse issues as specific foreign policy and specific agricultural proposals were contemplated. Advance copies of these addresses were disseminated to newsmen. Yet, when Wallace began to speak he soon responded to the interrelated pressures of the hecklers and the desires of his audience to hear him (1) run over the agitators—verbally, in the absence of a Presidential limousine, and (2) recite the litany of the faithful. For an account of these occasions see: *The New York Times*, October 8, 1968, p. 34. *The Pittsburgh Press*, October 22, 1968, p. 10. *The New York Times*, October 31, 1968, p. 38.

[3] As a mimetic-orator, Wallace's function as Edwin Black so insightfully describes it ". . . is not to shape an audience's beliefs and disbeliefs but to reflect them. He is the spokesman, official or unofficial, of some group in society, and his discourses may be taken as expressing the mind of that group." From Edwin Black, *Rhetorical Criticism: A Study in Method* (New York: The Macmillan Company, 1965), p. 167.

[4] This attitude was expressed in a televised interview among Wallace and some of his supporters which was seen on KDKA television, Channel 2, Pittsburgh, Pennsylvania, October 1, 1968.

[5] *The New York Times*, October 20, 1968, p. E15.

If the repetitiveness of Wallace's discourse was not discouraging to his followers, it was not exactly invigorating to the rhetorical critic. It is not that Wallace did not vary his speech—he did. Rather, it was the way in which he varied it. Imagine, if one will, a deck of fifty-two note-cards. Remove the first two and lay them aside. They represent Wallace's introductory remarks. Remove the last two note-cards and lay them aside. These cards contain Wallace's conclusion. Now thoroughly shuffle the remainder of the cards. Restack them in a randomized order with the introductory note-cards on the top of the deck and concluding note-cards on the bottom of the deck. Deliver the note-cards. (However, keep in mind that dealing off the bottom of the deck is permissible.) Repeat this procedure prior to the delivery of each speech. Occasionally, for the sake of variety, repeat the procedure while delivering the speech. The reader now has a rough approximation of Wallace's organization.

Within this framework, five issues characteristically appeared. Normally, one of these—race—was developed in what could be called the introduction of the address. Wallace liked to deal with the racial theme *per se* early in his speech. He usually offered the following disclaimer:

> I have never in my life made a *public statement*, in my political life, *calculated* to reflect upon anybody because of their race, color, creed, or national origin. [applause and cheers] And I don't intend to do so tonight [applause and cheers], and I never have. [applause, cheers, and usually a little foot stomping by now][6] (Italics mine.)

Having "dismissed" the racial question and shown to all present that he is not a racialist, Wallace would spend much of the rest of the evening talking about race, in terms of "law and order." It was almost as if he were practicing the suggestions for *insinuatio* outlined by the classical rhetoricians.

Slightly before, or after, the disclaimer Wallace would offer what could be interpreted as a thesis statement. The purpose of this address is to allow Wallace ". . . to give you our position again, as I have given it before in other parts of the country."[7] In no set order, the position followed. Usually, Wallace developed four additional issues: (1) anti-intellectualism, (2) law and order, (3) Vietnam, and (4) get "a dime's worth of difference."[8] The first three of these could loosely be construed as the main ideas or main points of the body of his speech. Typically, the transition into and statement of the first main idea (whichever it may have been) would read:

> What is another issue[9] that faces the American people? Now, first, the issue really, in the long run, generally speaking, is that we have a pseudo-

---

[6] This quotation in similar content, if not form, is found in all versions of the 1968 Presidential campaign speech to which this writer has listened. Hereafter, this particular address will be referred to as *The Speech*.

[7] *Ibid.*

[8] *Ibid.*

[9] Even though this may be the first issue of the body of the speech, Wallace might very well call it "another issue." This is really not incorrect as his racial disclaimer usually preceded all other issues. The terminology could be confusing to the rhetorical critic who is looking for an orderly, sequential flow of ideas. However, it did not seem to bother Wallace's audience who followed with great gusto and enthusiasm his freewheeling harangue from one brassy punch line to the next.

intellectual cult in our country. [applause] Now, I'm not talking about
the real intellectuals. We need the real intellectuals.[10]

The probative support, such as it was, would follow and Wallace would
race onward to the transition to the next main point—a transition which
sounded curiously like the last one (and the next one): "Now we have
got the other issue that confronts the people of our county and that is the
breakdown of law and order. (applause)"[11] What would follow would be
an attack on the Supreme Court, the Justice Department, big government
(which prevents mayors and governors from getting riot troops when they
need them), "pseudo-intellectuals" (again), "militants," "beatniks," "Communists," and "anarchists."

By now, the crowd is on its feet screaming and shouting their support
for Wallace and railing darkly at any anti-Wallace demonstrators who might
be present.

Between urging the audience to ". . . let the police handle it; let the
police handle it, Ladies and Gentlemen"[12,13] and blasting the demonstrators
with *ad Hominem* attacks ("Be good or we won't promote you to the second
grade." "You people use a lot of four letter words and call it freedom of
speech, but there are two words you people don't have in your vocabulary,
w-o-r-k and w-a-s-h." "Come on up here and I'll autograph your sandals
for you.")[14]; Wallace would be developing his third main idea: "Now
another issue that faces our people is the matter of Vietnam."[15] Within
this point sometimes certain subordinate concepts would become vaguely
apparent:

A.   . . . One thing we ought to do about involvement is make our friends go
     with us and help us [applause]—or stop foreign aid [applause] and make
     them pay back all the money they owe us from World War I right on up
     to the present. [much applause and cheers][16]
B.   . . . And second, we ought to lean heavily on the joint chiefs of staff.[17]
C.   . . . Another thing we ought to do is to . . . seek an indictment against
     these traitors [applause] and throw them under a good federal jail
     somewhere. [applause and cheers][18]

Once again, the lack of organization did not hamper the enjoyment of
the speech by Wallace's supporters. The impact of the complete discourse
would come across in some kind of a Gestalt whole. Suddenly, the message
is there. The listener is caught up and enmeshed in it, empathizing viscer-
ally with those around him and with the figure on stage whose head juts
above the big bullet-proof podium.

By now, Wallace has developed his fourth main idea. This is the fifth
issue with which he dealt and served as his conclusion. Get a dime's worth
of difference, he urged his followers, after all:

---

[10] *The Speech.*

[11] *Ibid.*

[12] *Ibid.*

[13] According to demonstrators with whom this writer has talked, the police, who
were probably pro-Wallace and/or anti-demonstrator, were more than happy to
"handle it."

[14] *The Speech.*

[15] *Ibid.*

[16] *Ibid.*

[17] *Ibid.*

[18] *Ibid.*

The National Republican Party leaders sound exactly almost like President Lyndon Johnson and the National Democrats. There is not a dime's worth of difference between them. And on January, 1969, if you put them in office you're going to be mad with them one week after the inauguration, but you got to wait four more years. So I say to you we must change for the purpose of changing trends—not just for the sake of changing. [applause and cheers][19]

This is the rhetoric of George Corley Wallace—a series of mangled metaphores,[20] mispronounced words, and loosely strung ideas. In short, a disconnected diatribe. Failures of disposition and style could be forgiven more easily if the speaker has had little or no exposure to the principles and practices of effective public speaking. George Wallace as a former debater,[21] a lawyer, and a politician can not make this claim. Despite this, however, Wallace was frequently successful in arousing his supporters to a fever pitch. This type of response is not at all inconsistent with the results one would expect from the speaking of a mimetic-orator. If Wallace had organized and delivered his speeches more effectively, he might well have succeeded in soliciting votes from members of the public outside of his hard core, mimetic following—votes necessary for greater political success in the 1968 Presidential campaign.

---

[19] *Ibid.*

[20] Several metaphors which Wallace used are striking; this one, however, is especially outstanding: "Those pointy-headed guideline writers have created a Frankenstein, and now their chickens are coming home to roost."

[21] *Candidates 1968* (Washington, D.C.: Congressional Quarterly Service, 1968), p. 90.

RICHARD M. NIXON'S INAUGURAL ADDRESS: A CRITICAL MOMENT IN HISTORY?

BERNARD L. BROCK*

> Each moment in history is a fleeting time, precious and unique.
> But some stand out as moments of beginning, in which courses are set
> that shape decades or centuries.
> This can be such a moment.[1]

With these words Richard M. Nixon launched his Inaugural Address which "in keeping with campaign promises and personal style . . . offered no new utopias, delivered no exhortations to grandeur."[2] Some critics praised Nixon for his eloquence, "There was a lift in his message—phrases of eloquence, phrases to raise the spirit, to enlarge hope. In this sense, it was a new Nixon as well as a new leader to whom we listened,"[3] while others focused on the thrust of his message, "peace and understanding." Yet, while listening to the address, one sensed an incompatibility between Nixon's grand purpose, setting a course for "decades or centuries," and his plain style, uneven tone and mixed metaphors.

However, after observing initial reactions, one is still left with the task of judging the address, so one asks, "What standards should be used in evaluating Nixon's Inaugural Address?" Should it be compared to past great inaugurals? Nixon encouraged this approach by comparing the present crisis to the one faced by Franklin Roosevelt in 1933 and by employing a style similar to John Kennedy's. Nixon did not create the same unity and mandate for personal action as did Franklin Roosevelt in his First Inaugural, but today the nation is not crippled by a "Great Depression" as it was in 1933. Nixon did not inspire the nation with a measured, high style as did John Kennedy, but neither does his ascent to the presidency provide the same stark contrast in style with his predecessor. The question is, "What made these speeches great?" Can one legitimately separate the address from the times and say definitely that it was the speech itself that was great, rather than the circumstances? No, one should not use the great addresses as the *standard* for evaluation.

Nixon's speech should be judged by standards appropriate to all inaugurals: "Was the address a meaningful response to immediate circumstances?" and "Did the address specify a positive direction for the new administration?" During the 1968 election, the nation had been divided between young and old, rich and poor, black and white, and doves and hawks, and these divisions contributed to Nixon's receiving a minority of the popular vote and failing to obtain a mandate from the people. Nixon had to acknowledge these divisions and respond in such a way as to capture the popular support that he was denied in the polls.

---

* Mr. Brock is Associate Professor of Speech, Communication, and Theatre Arts and Director of Forensics at the University of Minnesota.

[1] All quotations from this speech are from "Nixon's Inaugural Address," *U. S. Congressional Record*, 91st Cong., 1st Sess., January 20, 1969, S561–561.

[2] "Nixon's Message: 'Let us Gather in Light,'" *Time*, Vol. 93, No. 4 (January 24, 1969), 9.

[3] The editorial from January 21, 1969, Memphis (Tenn.) Press-Scimitar was read into the *Congressional Record* on January 27, 1969, 91st Cong., 1st Sess., E491.

Nixon attempted this in the introduction as he tied the occasion and unity together: "I ask you to share with me today the majesty of this moment. In the orderly transfer of power, we celebrate the unity that keeps us free." The idea of unity and freedom was extended as Nixon discussed the difficulty of attaining peace as we approach "the third millennium." Nixon's strategy was to transcend these divisions by calling for peace.

But he returns to the divisions in recognizing "a crisis of the spirit":

> We find ourselves rich in goods but ragged in spirit, reaching with magnificient precision for the moon but falling into raucous discord on earth.
>
> We are caught in war, wanting peace. We are torn by division, wanting unity. We see around us empty lives wanting fulfillment. We see tasks that need doing waiting for hands to do them.
>
> To a crisis of the spirit, we need an answer of the spirit.

Having acknowledged the divisions, Nixon recommended a solution which would result in unity and would suggest a popular mandate, "We cannot learn from one another until we stop shouting at one another. . . ."

Nixon continued to pursue unity and a mandate in considering the "role of government and people." He promised that "government will listen" to all the people—especially "those who have been left out" and "those left behind." At this point Nixon's call for a mandate became stronger:

> What has to be done has to be done by government and people together or it will not be done at all. The lesson of past agony is that without the people we can do nothing, with the people we can do everything . . . we can build a great cathedral of the spirit—each of us raising it one stone at a time as he reaches out to his neighbor, helping, caring, doing.

One can see how the old, the rich, the white, and the hawks could identify with Nixon's transcendent appeal, "a great cathedral of the spirit," but one questions its acceptability to the young, the poor, the black, and the doves who are all *shouting* for tangible actions.

Later Nixon adds, "we shall promise only what we know we can produce," and "the laws have caught up with our conscience." Nixon has not offered much hope to the disenchanted. Also, one must remember Nixon's conclusion to the "crisis of the spirit": "We cannot learn from one another until we stop shouting at one another. . . ." He might as well have told the underprivileged to stop demonstrating and criticizing the establishment.

Yes, Nixon did bid for unity, but beyond a few clichés he offered nothing which would have gained this unity. Nixon did not provide a meaningful response to the immediate circumstances of division.

But the question remains, "Did the address point a positive direction for the new administration?" The answer was partially provided when we discovered that Nixon did not provide much hope for those left out of our "Great Society."

The ritualistic character of the Inaugural Address and Nixon's superficial attempts at unity make identifying a definite future course difficult. Yet, some signs stand out. Nixon clearly envisions his administration as being critical in gaining world peace:

> For the first time, because the people of the world want peace and the leaders of the world are afraid of war, the times are on the side of peace. . . .

> What kind of a nation we will be, what kind of a world we will live in, whether we shape the future in the image of our hopes, is ours to determine by our actions and our choices.

In fact, peace becomes the major goal of his administration:

> Let us take as our goal: Where peace is unknown, make it welcome; where peace is fragile, make it strong; where peace is temporary, make it permanent.
> After a period of confrontation, we are entering an era of negotiation.

So the direction for Nixon's administration is toward world peace during an era of negotiation. During this period Nixon will preside, and he will be known as the peace-maker, "the greatest honor history can bestow." Nixon will be operating in a world which he feels he knows quite well: "I have come to know the leaders of the world, and the great forces, the hatreds, the fears, that divide the world," and a world that he dwarfs by citing the words of Archibald MacLeish:

> To see the earth as it truly is, small and blue and beautiful in that eternal silence where it floats, is to see ourselves as riders on the earth together, brothers on that bright loveliness in the eternal cold—brothers who know now they are truly brothers.

Thus, Nixon concludes, "our destiny lies not in the stars but on earth itself, in our own hands, in our own hearts." Nixon's Inaugural Address suggests that he sees himself as the peace-maker who will personally assure world peace for "decades or centuries."

One immediately questions whether Nixon could believe a single person could be the crucial ingredient in obtaining world peace, but a quick look at his political background suggests this may be possible. In 1952, when public opinion was running against him because of a questionable use of political funds and Eisenhower was considering dropping him as the vice-presidential candidate, Nixon appeared on national television and presented his now famous "Checkers Speech" which reversed the tide and insured his candidacy. Then in 1960, when Rockefeller emerged as a threat to Nixon's presidential hopes, Nixon personally negotiated crucial platform issues with Rockefeller and demanded their acceptance from the platform committee at the convention. Finally after 1962, when Nixon committed political suicide by lashing out at the press and by announcing his permanent retirement from politics, he made a personal comeback through tireless campaigning for Republican candidates across the country resulting in his 1968 presidential nomination which symbolized his personal victory. These incidents suggest as does his autobiography, Six Crises,[4] that Nixon's political history is one of personal victories and defeats, so one should not be surprised to see him view world peace in personal terms.

Nixon's Inaugural Address suggests that the thrust of his administration will be toward *personal* negotiation for peace, and this direction is consistent with his campaign talk of summit conferences with world leaders. Still one must ask whether the final third of this century, the era of negotiation, requires a president who creates world conditions or one who responds intelligently to them. Is it possible that Nixon in evaluating the circumstances would over-value the role played by a single individual? His predecessor made that mistake. In 1964 Johnson saw the futility of military

---

[4] Richard M. Nixon, Six Crises (New York: Doubleday & Co., 1962).

involvement in Asia. But later, he overestimated his power to control circumstances, and he escalated United States involvement in Vietnam and caused his own political demise. Johnson, like Nixon, viewed politics personally. So to the extent that Nixon's Inaugural Address points a direction for his administration, it raises the question of whether Nixon, failing to profit from Johnson's mistakes, over-values the role the president can play in world politics.

Nixon's Inaugural Address will not go down in history for its eloquent style, nor will it generate the much-needed support from the rejected of society. But it does suggest a direction for his administration. It indicates a period of personal diplomacy. We all hope at this critical moment in history that Nixon does not follow the course set by Lyndon Johnson and implied in Nixon's inaugural and that he was right when he said, "the times are on the side of peace."

DEAN RUSK: A DIALOGUE AT INDIANA UNIVERSITY

Uvieja Good*

When Dean Rusk visited Indiana University on Tuesday, October 31, 1967, to speak to the students and faculty, objectors of the Johnson Administration's Vietnam policy planned to show opposition to Rusk's warmonger image. Knowing well his actions in the recent war years and knowing that "because of the policy he symbolizes, hundreds of men will probably be killed in the next year or so,"[1] the campus thoroughly prepared for his arrival.

For a long time Ernest K. Lindley, a former Indiana University student now in the State Department, repeatedly urged Rusk to speak at Indiana University. After Rusk accepted an October 30 speaking engagement at Columbus, Indiana, Lindley persuaded him to speak at his nearby alma mater the following day. When the Convocations Committee received notice of the invitation, they recognized the honor of having such a distinguished speaker and agreed to sponsor his visit.[2]

The announcement of Rusk's visit initially aroused no anticipation of trouble among the majority of the students or campus authorities. His visit was considered by them to be an honor to the University. No responsible authority early recognized the disruptive influence Rusk would have on the campus; few visualized the need for extensive security and certainly few suspected the trouble that would storm the campus.[3]

When the students learned of Rusk's visit, the reaction of members of the "liberal left" was not subtle. The student leaders of the movement, David Cahill, Russell Block, and Guy Loftman, reproached Professor Reed Dickerson, Chairman of the Convocations Committee, condemning him for scheduling in the past two years a "parade of hawks." They listed Richard Nixon, General Maxwell Taylor, General Lewis Hershey, Hubert Humphrey, and Senator Wayne Morse, the only "dove." They then urged the Committee to secure before October 31, a nationally prominent speaker opposed to the war in Vietnam to address the campus before January 1, 1968 (but not within two days of a vacation). If the Committee should find this impossible, they demanded a cancellation of the Secretary of State's invitation to speak.[4]

Professor Dickerson conceded that, although unintentional, an imbalance had in fact developed. He explained, however, that it is impossible to audit any speaker before he appears; and, thus, the Committee often does not know what position a scheduled speaker might take.[5]

To partially correct the imbalance, the Committee scheduled an anti-war speaker, Boston University professor of government Howard Zinn, to speak

---

* Miss Good is a graduate student at Indiana University.

[1] *Indiana Daily Student* (Bloomington), November 4, 1967, p. 4.

[2] Interview with Professor Reed Dickerson, Chairman of the Convocation Committee and Professor of Law at Indiana University, May 7, 1968; *Indiana Daily Student*, October 4, 1967, p. 1 and October 31, 1967, p. 4.

[3] Interview with Professor Reed Dickerson; letter to Dean Shaffer, Dean of Students, Indiana University, May 8, 1968.

[4] *Indiana Daily Student*, October 26, 1967, p. 1 and October 31, 1967, p. 4; Interview with Professor Reed Dickerson.

[5] Interview with Professor Reed Dickerson.

on December 1, 1967. At the announcement of this invitation, the leaders of Students for a Democratic Society (SDS) and Committee to End the War in Vietnam (CEWV) made no agreement with the Convocation Committee to prevent interference with Rusk's speech. Block assured the Committee that *he* would cause no trouble but explained that he did not know what his followers might do. He knew demonstrations would be staged, for a person of Mr. Rusk's stature must expect these when he speaks, but Block hoped they would be orderly.[6]

Nearly 120 police authorities began preparation for Rusk's visit. Soon after Rusk accepted the invitation to speak, two of his advance men approached Captain Spannuth, Chief of the Safety Division at Indiana University. They instructed him in all of the usual security precautions for Rusk's visit. Since the University and city police forces did not have enough men to cover the event, they requested the assistance of state patrolmen. "Plain clothes" men were scattered throughout the audience and at other pertinent points. Men guarded all doors leading into the auditorium and all entrances onto the stage. No one would be permitted backstage without first presenting a special button of authorization. Even with all of the University's security preparations, Rusk's personal security team accompanied him.[7]

On the day before Rusk's speech, the "Dean Rusk welcoming committee" (CEWV) collected approximately 130 students and began distributing leaflets throughout the campus with instructions on how to show opposition to the Johnson administration's policy in Vietnam during Rusk's speech. According to Russell Block, the "number one" instruction was "Do not stop him from speaking."[8] They urged dissenters to wear "peace" armbands, to enter the auditorium as early as possible and to heckle Rusk with appropriate comments when they disagreed.[9] Don Kaplan, president of SDS, instructed interested individuals to demonstrate with faculty members in front of the auditorium.[10]

Soon the excitement caused supporters of the Administration's policy in Vietnam to begin preparations for a counter-demonstration. Robert Tyrell, a member of the State Executive Committee of Young Americans for Freedom, instructed people wishing to counter-demonstrate to dress in coat and tie and meet at 9:45 a.m., October 31, to march around Showalter Fountain in front of the auditorium. At 10:00, as many as possible were to go inside, take seats and applaud when dissenters booed and hissed. An estimate revealed that nearly 2,000 of Tyrell's demonstrators were left outside the auditorium.[11]

On the morning of October 31, an editorial in the *Indiana Daily Student* welcomed Mr. Rusk and encouraged all readers, regardless of political view, to attend the event. A satire appeared in the same issue encouraging dissenters to go to Dunn Meadow (a plot of ground set aside for demonstrations), dance around the flag and take out their frustrations on one

---

[6] *Indiana Daily Student*, October 27, 1967, p. 1; interview with Professor Reed Dickerson.

[7] Interview with Captain William G. Spannuth, May 13, 1968.

[8] Interview with Russell Block, May 6, 1968.

[9] *Ibid.*

[10] *Bloomington Herald-Telegram*, October 30, 1967, p. 1.

[11] *Indiana Daily Student*, October 31, 1967; interview with Robert Tyrell, May 10, 1968.

another so that the rest could hear Rusk's speech. "Let's let Mr. Rusk go back to Washington untarred-and-feathered."[12] Another student expressed concern wondering ". . . what sort of shame will be cast upon the entire student body by the probable infantile demonstrations. . . ."[13]

Under cloudy skies, demonstrators and counter-demonstrators awaited Rusk's arrival. At 9:45 a.m. an anxious audience occupied all 3,738 seats in the auditorium.[14] At 10:30 applause accompanied the shouts and boos of about 200 anti-war demonstrators, and signs reading "BOMB HANOI NOW," and "VICTORY IN VIETNAM" greeted Dean Rusk, Secretary of State, to Indiana University.[15]

Rusk began his speech, and his dialogue, immediately after President Starr introduced him. Distinct boos and shouts of "Eichmann," "murder," "Fascist" and "grow up," molded the first line of his address: "Thank you for letting me be your Halloween guest today." An audience member responded with, "There're enough ghosts with you." When Rusk explained the nature of his invitation to speak at Indiana University, someone from the audience clearly suggested, "You invited yourself."

The audience shouted and booed throughout Rusk's next sentence to the end of the first paragraph. In that period of four sentences, the audience had completely disrupted Rusk six times with shouts lasting from 7 to 15 seconds. The Secretary decided to deal with the interruptions immediately.

> Let us be clear about one thing, and I want to be as gentle as possible in making this remark, that it's been a long time since Mr. Khrushchev banged his shoe on the table at the United Nations. I am prepared to be your guest. I am not going to engage in a shouting match with anyone.

Applause, accompanied with "name calling," thundered for 38 seconds.

His reference to Khruschchev had not brought the group under control. With irritation evident in his voice, he made a second attempt to "set things straight," forcing more shouts from the audience.

> I think—I think you ought to know that—that in all—in all of our discussions, Mr. Gromyko and I treat each other with the greatest of possible personal courtesy. And if that—and if that were not so—if that were not so, peace would be far more difficult than it is today.

He immediately returned to his prepared speech. He thanked the University for its contributions to peace and without hesitation apologized to the press for not giving them an advance copy of his speech. He said he wanted to talk personally and informally to the audience. He appeared to want to use a manuscript speech—but the nature and activities of the audience altered those plans, for it became clear that he could not follow any planned sequence of thought.

He then stated that the United States must "think long and hard about how we build a powerful peace in the World." Probably in response to audience jeers, he expressed hope that those present could at least agree that that was the central question, "despite differences of view about how we get there. . . ." To shouts of "drop the bomb," and "it's wrong," he faltered: "I'll—I'll—come—I'll come to that—I'll come to that."

---

[12] *Indiana Daily Student*, October 31, 1967, p. 1.

[13] *Ibid*, October 28, 1967.

[14] *Indiana Daily Student*, November 1, 1967, p. 1.

[15] *Ibid*. The following quotations have been taken from a tape recording of the event at Indiana University.

Rusk explained that the older generation may have made mistakes, but they have also gained experience; however, the younger generation could supply "fresh hopes" to old ideas. The audience interjected shouts throughout the explanation.

As he began to develop the history of the framing of the United Nations Charter in 1945, the audience started its own dialogue: "Shut up and let him talk." He appeased the audience by asking them to "re-read" Article One of the United Nations' Charter. Then he related selected acts of aggression starting with World War I, associating each with the appropriate periods in his life. Throughout this portion of the speech were shouts of "napalm," "Fascist," "like us," and "just like the Americans went into Vietnam."

After relating incidents since 1945 that proved the power of Article One of the United Nations' Charter, shouts began again: "What about Cuba?", "We're her ally!", "Where is the United Nations?" Rusk commented, "We'll have a question time in a moment." This initiated 17 seconds of applause, shouts, and laughter.

After 11 minutes of speaking, Rusk explicitly used the word "Vietnam" for the first time. He claimed that the Vietnamese issue "has to do with the prospect of organizing peace throughout the vast Pacific area . . ." an area in which the United States has alliances with several other countries. He said, "If we are to prevent war, those who might become our adversaries must know in advance that these alliances mean what they say." An 18 second interruption of applause, mixed with boos and shouts, followed.

Rusk explained the importance of maintaining the treaties and then viewed "South Vietnam specifically on a number of points." We are there because of the North Vietnamese's aggression; we have attempted to bargain with Hanoi; we need to settle division by peace not violence. Hecklers continued their efforts.

He proceeded: "Now as to negotiations," and was interrupted by shouts: "Now, now!" "What about NLF?" Rusk reacted with "I agree, now." He claimed that he will meet Hanoi in any capital to talk peace. Again a dissenter shouted, "What about the NLF?" Rusk responded:

> As far as the NLF is concerned, President Johnson has said that obtaining the view of the NLF is not an insuperable problem in negotiations. I am prepared to negotiate that point with someone who can stop the bombing. There is no point in my negotiating with you. . . . We are prepared to negotiate today without any conditions whatever.

Six seconds of shouting halted Rusk. He explained that the United States wanted to talk, but Hanoi first wants a "permanent and unconditional cessation of bombing of the North. At this point, a wild outbreak of shouting seized the audience. For 40 seconds they booed, applauded, and shouted, "Why don't you do it?" This dissension forced Dean Rusk to clarify the situation with an analogy.

> I am sure you would agree that if we said there could be talks only if all the violence in South Vietnam stopped while we continued to bomb the North, you would say that we are crazy. Why then—why then does it appear to be a reasonable proposition when North Vietnam makes exactly the same proposal in reverse?

Hecklers shouted "It's their country." "Get out." Again he exclaimed that we are prepared to talk peace.

Finally he turned to the word "escalation" which precipitated another dialogue with the audience. A shout rang from the audience: "It's your word." Rusk contended that everything we do in Vietnam is tagged escalation; no one calls any advancements by North Vietnamese escalation. In this explanation he stated: "Today North Vietnamese and Viet Cong forces are in Cambodia." When a heckler shouted, "So are ours," Rusk answered, "There're no—there're no American forces in Cambodia." After a dissenter retorted, "Lies," Rusk continued: "Their moving into Cambodia has not been called escalation." The crowd interrupted again: "Why not!" "It's their country!" Hearty applause started while Rusk made another attempt to speak: "It is the country of . . ." again applause drowned his words. "Seventeen million South Vietnamese have a rather different view of whose country it is." Stronger shouts started: "It's not our country." "If you wanta' go, I'll buy you a ticket." After 25 seconds of shouts, laughter, applause, audience dialogue, and Rusk's contemplation of temper control, he calmly turned to Doctor Starr: "President Starr, this . . . makes me rather anxious to get to the question and answer time. Suppose we start that right now."

President Starr attempted to shame the group by referring to the University's tradition of free speech and pointing out that many wanted to listen and that no one had to remain. He then called for questions. The shouts continued, although less severe, throughout the question and answer period.

At one point during the question period, a lady hit a heckler with her umbrella, causing the audience to break into a chant of "Hit him again, harder, harder," followed by 50 seconds of applause.

At the conclusion of the question period, Rusk thanked the group before making his departure.

> I have some letters from a number of you before I came up here, letters from some who are supporting us in Vietnam and some who were opposing in Vietnam. But . . . both letters told me that I would have a warm welcome. You've not disappointed me. Thank you very much ladies and gentlemen.

The audience applauded and shouted strongly for 22 seconds during a standing ovation.

Rusk seemed to invite his treatment throughout the speech. He spoke deliberately, pausing often as though he were deciding whether or not to continue speaking. These pauses afforded an agreeable environment for hecklers in the audience. Some pauses were so long that one wondered if he had finished speaking.

His style bears the marks of a politician. He was evasive and wordy, and covered few major points. Rusk employed occasional analogies, often used repetition and tried to secure identification with his audience. He frequently repeated the phrase, "think long and hard," once deviating to "think long and soberly." He emphasized by prolonging the [o] sound in "long," and trilling the [r] in "hard." As the audience anticipated, he brought with him no new ideas, and they were prepared for his old remarks.

After his speech, policemen standing shoulder-to-shoulder helped Rusk to a waiting car. Supporting demonstrators tried to surround Rusk for protection.[16] There were no attempts to harm Secretary Rusk; however,

---

[16] Interview with Robert Tyrell.

one girl broke through the line and threw herself in front of a police car. An officer removed her from the path of the car.[17]

Although University officials anticipated the possibility of violence, they were greatly relieved when the dissension went no further than noise.[18] Russell Block claims that his group carried out plans to precision, and Robert Tyrell feels his group performed well too.[19]

Some people felt apologetic. Some complained that they did not get to hear Rusk's complete speech while others contended that Rusk said what he would have said anyhow. Tony Allen, an Indiana University student, made a distinction between two types of heckling: one keeps a person from making his point; the other does not. The latter, he believed, characterized Rusk's speech.[20]

Because of Rusk's increasing war image and his experiences with other anti-war groups, he was not surprised with the demonstrators at Indiana University. One may even contend that Rusk felt a sense of accomplishment. There were basically three distinct groups that heard his speech; one group was anti-war; one pro-war; and the third was neutral. When hecklers interrupted Rusk, many neutrals became sympathetic. Although the purpose of the demonstrations was probably not to win members for each group, at the end of Rusk's speech, the counter-demonstrators had undoubtedly won the support of many more neutrals than the anti-war demonstrators had won. Anti-war demonstrators did not completely defeat Rusk, for when he left Indiana University Dean Rusk had far more sympathizers than when he arrived.

---

[17] *Indiana Daily Student*, November 1, 1967, p. 1.

[18] *Indianapolis Star*, November 1, 1967, p. 6.

[19] Interviews with Robert Tyrell and Russell Block.

[20] *Indiana Daily Student*, November 1, 1967, p. 4.

THE NIXON CAMPAIGN

WAYNE C. EUBANK

I.

"The time has come for us to leave the valley of despair and climb the mountain, so that we may see the glory of the dawn, a new day for America, a new dawn for peace and freedom to the world."[1]

With this admonition, Mr. Nixon challenged the American people to join him in the great adventure: the establishment of peace at home, the establishment of peace abroad.

James Perry, writing in *The National Observer*, declared, "Mr. Nixon's acceptance speech was, in fact, a polished version of a basic speech familiar to every reporter who has travelled with him."[2]

The speech, effectively delivered, which seemed to match the mood of the convention, was loaded with accusations, declarations, generalizations, and emotional proof. The Nixon strategy was clear: attack, take the offensive and keep it, awaken the American people to the dangers at home and abroad, and blame both conditions on the Johnson–Humphrey administration. Two major issues rang through the speech: law and order with justice at home, the establishing of peace and national integrity, abroad.

II. UNITY

Although tempers flared occasionally, there was no real bloodletting at the Republican convention in Miami. Uniting the few disenchanted was relatively easy for Nixon. He lost no time in launching the Republican "love-in." The week following the Miami convention, Nixon, his top advisors, and colleagues met in California to plan the strategy necessary for Republican unity and a campaign victory. Upon departing from California, Nixon engaged in a three-day "whirlwind trip wooing Republican moderates in the large states of the industrial Northeast."[3] Quickly the Three R's (Rockefeller, Reagan, Romney) took the pledge. In rapid succession followed big-state governors and such notables as Mayor Lindsay and Senator Edward Brooke.

Insured of party unity, Nixon retired to Florida. "As he sopped up the sun in Key Biscayne and waited for the Democrats to nominate his opponent, Richard Nixon could only hope to be as successful during his next venture in courtship—when he sets out to kindle a love affair with the American people."[4]

III. ELECTORAL VOTE STRATEGY

Traditionally, a Republican presidential candidate wins by building a strong voter support in the Midwest and mountain states and then achieving victory in at least five of the "big seven" states—New York, Pennsylvania,

Wayne C. Eubank is Professor of Speech at The University of New Mexico.

[1] *Vital Speeches*, September 1, 1968, p. 677.

[2] *The National Observer*, August 12, 1968, p. 12.

[3] *Newsweek*, September 2, 1968, p. 32.

[4] *Newsweek*, September 2, 1968, p. 33.

Michigan, Texas, Ohio, Illinois, and California—which carry 210 electoral votes. Uncertain of carrying five of the "big seven" states (he only carried three), Nixon and his staff devised a new strategy for victory. Writing off four states of the Deep South to Wallace (Louisiana, Mississippi, Alabama, and Georgia), he would concentrate on the new south-border section (nine states—Florida, South Carolina, North Carolina, Virginia, West Virginia, Kentucky, Tennessee, Oklahoma, and Texas)—he actually won seven of the nine. This strategy was the primary reason for Agnew's choice as a running mate. He was highly acceptable to the south-border section and not meaningfully offensive to the midwest and mountain states. With this strategy, Nixon was able to lose four of the "big seven" states—New York, Pennsylvania, Michigan, and Texas—and still win.

IV. RADIO–TV AND ELECTRONICS IN THE CAMPAIGN
or NIXON'S MIXED MEDIA BAG

A. *Talking Papers*

Customarily, presidential candidates are expected to issue a *position paper* which states their stand on a wide range of issues. Such a publication often gets lost in the heat of the campaign and usually has little real value. In lieu of such a paper, which he had issued in 1960, Nixon came up with a political first in his "talking papers." This technique consisted of a series of fifteen radio talks "covering the gamut from national resources to problems of senior citizens." The "talking paper" that attracted the widest and most favorable attention was entitled "The Presidency," in which Mr. Nixon advanced his conception of the office and incidentally his philosophy of government. Estimates of total listeners during the 15 "talking papers" ran as high as 7,500,000.[5]

Following each broadcast, the speech was reprinted in pamphlet form and distributed by Nixon's information centers.

B. *TV Spots*

Early in September, considerably in advance of the Democratic soft-sell commercials, one-minute Nixon spots were introduced on T.V. In the main, they were hard-hitting quotations taken from Nixon's acceptance speech "interspersed with crowd applause and all ending with waving, white-on-red 'Nixon's the One' placards filling the screen."[6] Forty to fifty such spots were employed during the campaign. These shorts—a few were longer than one minute—focused on the candidate Mr. Nixon, his face and voice. In contrast, the Democratic spots focused on the message rather than the candidate.

C. *The Richard Nixon Show*

The idea of a candidate–question panel television show grew out of the New Hampshire primary where Mr. Nixon had "head to head" talks with a representative group of citizens, usually about six, with no studio audience. The half-hour talks were taped for later showing and used in other states prior to the Miami convention. Following the convention, Mr. Shakespeare, a vice president on leave from CBS, lengthened the show to

---

[5] *Newsweek*, November 4, 1968, p. 28.

[6] *New York Times*, October 1, 1968, p. 32.

one hour and included a studio audience of about 200 selected loyal Republicans. The quiz panel usually consisted of about seven members—primarily Republican with some Democrat and Independent representation. Efforts were made to provide a fair cross-section on the panel. The Richard Nixon Show, always televised in a large city, received excellent response—particularly, it was thought, among dissident Democrats and Independents.

D. *The Neo-Psychedelic Campus Pitch*

Seeking to capture the attention and support of the voting-age college student, Mort Allen of the Youth for Nixon Committee contracted with Jimini Products of California to produce a psychedelic poster in rainbow colors to brighten Mr. Nixon's image. "Under the legend 'Nixon's the One' the central motif is a broad, smiling charcoal sketch of the candidate, leading a throng of celebrated supporters ranging from Senator Dirksen to Anita Ekberg."[7] The initial printing was 25,000. These posters were distributed on major college campuses for one dollar each.

E. *Electronic Aids*

Under the Citizens for Nixon "Participation Politics" program, thousands of citizens talked with Mr. Nixon each day. "The 'Speak to Nixon' Program . . . invites voters to say whatever is on their mind on tape recordings that will reach the Republican presidential candidate and key staff members.

"Every person who accepts this invitation gets a reply from the candidate, punched out by a trained staff from a battery of computers that have in their memory bank 67 Nixon positions on the key issues, drawn from speeches and writings.

"The computers, keyed to electronically controlled typewriters, produce individual answers responding to the questions. . . ."[8]

An electronic signature machine adds "Richard M. Nixon."

This new technique, another campaign first for Nixon, was also used to isolate the issues that voters were thinking about in various sections of the country. This phase was called "Listening Post." A statistic section, the third element in the "Participation Politics" program, tabulated the issues foremost in the thinking of the public week by week. The findings were transmitted directly to Mitchell, campaign chairman, or Klein, communications manager. They in turn informed Mr. Nixon of the hot issue of the week. For example: law and order, a strong issue in September, had dropped to 12% by October 11. Foreign policy, triggered by the Czech crisis, had jumped to 40% by October 11.

In a more personal fashion, Mr. Nixon has utilized a brave new world of gadgetry. During a motorcade in transit, chatting with farmers in California, Nixon need only reach for the "Briefcase"—the handy leatherette case containing a cordless mobile radio telephone. The "Briefcase" enables Nixon and staff to remain in constant contact with aides in New York and Washington.[9]

"The Nixonite's other favorite gadget is the 'Magic Carpet,' a portable telecopier over which New York (headquarters) can transmit news stories,

---

[7] *New York Times*, October 9, 1968, p. 35.

[8] *New York Times*, October 21, 1968, p. C38.

[9] *Newsweek*, September 30, 1968, p. 28.

letters, and other materials to the touring team wherever it is. . . . Nixon's number one campaign jet also boasts an air-to-ground telephone . . . and a telephone-linked teleprinter capable of sending and receiving in the air."[10]

Mr. Nixon's politico–cybernetic system was located in the Willard Hotel, Washington. There 600 full-time employees plus some 1300 part-time volunteers meet the public and man the machines.

"The Nixonites have put on magnetic tape more than 1,100,000 names and addresses of a reserve army of workers. National director, John Warner, says his goal is 5,000,000 names by November 5. Within 72 hours, Warner boasts, leased computers across the nation can crank out five million letters."[11]

V. THE STANDARD OR CAMPAIGN SPEECH

Nixon's campaign speech was composed primarily of a restatement of the issues in his acceptance speech. The issues were not discussed in a substantive way; rather, Mr. Nixon clung rather closely to a variety of tried and true applause lines on the issues. As *Newsweek* pointed out near the end of the campaign, "The set speech that Nixon delivers at one hermetic rally after another is much like cotton candy, long on promises and all but devoid of particulars."[12] For want of a better term, I call this "sloganeering."

The following examples illustrate Mr. Nixon's sloganeering on most of the major issues:

On Vietnam: "We will bring the war to an honorable conclusion." "I belong to a party that ended one war and kept us out of war for eight years."

On Washington: "The crime capital of the world."

On law and order: "The first civil right of every American is to be free from domestic violence."

On lack of respect for America abroad: "The American flag isn't going to be a doormat for anyone when we get into the White House."

On social justice: "Progress without order is tyranny."

On time for a change: "Let's not send in the old team for a new job." "We can't be led into the 70's by the men who stumbled into the 60's." "When you're in trouble, you don't turn to the men who got you in trouble to get you out of it."

On the administration's poverty programs: "We are going to take millions off welfare rolls and put them on payrolls."

On Democratic party disunity: "A party which cannot unify itself cannot unify our nation."

On America's future under the Republicans: "Prosperity without war, progress without inflation."

On Nixon's credibility: "I will never promise what I can't deliver."

On Humphrey: "The fastest, loosest tongue in America."

And, of course, the kicky slogan of Nixon, the fighter, and the motif of the Republican campaign of 1968: "We're going to sock it to 'em."

VI. EFFICIENCY OF CAMPAIGN MECHANICS

Midway through the campaign, *Time* magazine declared, "Smooth as a space satellite, precise as a computer, the 1968 Nixon-mobile whirs around

---

[10] *Newsweek*, September 30, 1968, p. 28.

[11] *Time*, October 25, 1968, p. 26.

[12] *Newsweek*, October 21, 1968, p. 31.

the country like a politician's dream machine. The candidate is seldom more than ten minutes late for an appearance. The bands strike up on cue; balloons tumble down at just the right moment. Meticulous planning schedules put the nominee at just the place where the turn-out will be largest and the crowd will be the most responsive."[13]

During the final week of the campaign, *Newsweek* observed regarding Nixon's preplanning, "The speech is always well received because it is almost always given to a carefully recruited rally of the faithful drummed up by a hard-eyed team of 75 advance men, especially trained and armed with a 75-page manual on crowdsmanship."[14]

Time correspondent Simmons Fentress, assigned to the Nixon campaign, declared, "You do get the feeling that Nixon's campaign is as carefully planned as the Normandy invasion."[15]

The campaign was really rather paradoxical. Nixon's stumping was programmed to project the feeling of intensity, vitality, and sweep; however, for the candidate it was a rather leisurely affair. Nixon's strategy board carefully booked his appearances in order to avoid over-exposure or over-exhaustion. He seldom missed a regular night's sleep and spent several of the campaign weekends relaxing in the sun. The mad race of the 1960 campaign, when he visited every state in the union, was missing. In 1968 he covered 31 states, confining his appearances primarily to large population centers. Practically all of the 50,000 miles travelled was in a luxury fleet of Boeing 727's.

VII. INTO THE STRETCH

During most of the campaign, the Nixon staff had purposely shielded him from unstaged, open appearances. Most of his public speeches were delivered in a carefully set atmosphere. Open radio and television appearances, with trained newspaper men, had been ruled out in favor of television question and answer sessions with local people. Only during the last week of the campaign did the Nixon strategists really open their candidate to the public in such presentations as "Meet the Press," "Face the Nation," and the election eve television telethon—incidentally or intentionally—without the presence of his running mate.

SUMMARY

On August 8, 1968, with the ringing phrase, "We're going to sock it to 'em this year," Richard Nixon vowed to bring "law and order with justice at home" and "restore peace and national integrity abroad." Within ten days following the Miami convention Nixon had solidified the main forces in the Republican party. If a few hold-outs needed a nudge, the unfolding horror of disunity in the Chicago Democratic convention sent them racing for the unity bandwagon.

Denying the accepted Republican formula for victory, the Nixon team chartered a new strategy. Instead of building a voter base in the midwest and mountain states and then trying to win at least five of the "Big Seven," the Nixon electoral strategy lay in courting the new south-border states with

---

[13] *Time*, September 27, 1968, p. 18.
[14] *Newsweek*, November 4, 1968, p. 28.
[15] *Time*, October 18, 1968, p. 23.

their 127 electoral votes. Nixon was right. He carried only three of the "Big Seven" but seven of the nine south-border states, which insured the victory.

"Fantastic" describes the Nixonite's employment of electronics during the campaign. Electronic firsts for the Nixon campaign were: "Talking Papers," "Participation Politics Program," the "Psychedelic Poster Campus Campaign," the "Magic Carpet," the "Briefcase," and the wide use of computers at the Willard Hotel headquarters in Washington.

Long before the Democratic campaign program emerged, hard-hitting television spots, taken from Nixon's acceptance speech, were a steady household diet.

The "T.V. Panel–Question Show" insured Mr. Nixon of a partisan studio audience and a relatively friendly panel. Developed through months of campaigning prior to the convention, the Nixon stump speech advanced the issues presented in his acceptance speech—less through solid forms of support than by fool-proof applause phrases which may be labeled "slogan-eering."

The Nixon campaign was a technical masterpiece, "a triumph of the politics of methodology." A 350-man advertising staff, dedicated to the technical mastery of campaigning, gave Mr. Nixon the best merchandising a presidential candidate has received.

Is there really a new Nixon? I don't think so. Certainly his last four years on the resurrection road have brought change. He is more confident, more objective, more mature, far better equipped to be President than in 1960. The campaign victory certainly established him as an adroit political technician. In his "talking speech" on "The Presidency," Mr. Nixon declared, "The President must articulate the nation's values, define its goals, and marshal its will." To achieve this purpose he must rally the American people. Near the end of the campaign he stated, "I intend to get the very best men and women I can find in this country and give them responsibility." I can think of no wiser action, no surer formula for success on the part of a minority President than the assembling of a genuine coalition government.

Mr. Nixon did a masterful job of putting a party and a presidential campaign together. We hope that he will be as astute in wedding his American dream to the American people.

THE BALLOT OR THE BULLET: ONE-MAN DIALECTIC

PEGGY REYNOLDS

The mid-1960's marks an era of turbulence in the black man's struggle to assert his individuality within the framework of the American domestic scene. It is an era in which white liberals began abortive efforts at legislating a civil rights 'conscience'; and in which black men began turning to articulate, outspoken 'Negro leaders' to pave the way to a more meaningful concept of community. It is an era characterized by transition, in which the black man not only proclaimed his revolt against the role of eunuch in a WASP society, but began to make himself heard above the din of 'do-gooding.' It marks, as well, a transition in strategic emphasis from passivity and nonviolence to militance.

Inextricably bound up with this transitory period is the figure of Malcolm X. Although seldom associated with the current Black Power furor, his shifting ideologies and personal crises reflect, on a number of levels, its tumultuous beginnings.

On March 8, 1964, Malcolm X, who had been indisputably considered the Black Muslim movement's "second-in-command,"[1] and had risen to prominence as *the* spokesman for Elijah Muhammad (founder of the Nation of Islam), declared his withdrawal from the organization. In the ensuing brief span of time before his assassination in 1965 he managed to immerse himself in the civil rights controversy, to establish his own organization (Muslim Mosque Inc.), to make a pilgrimage to Mecca which significantly altered the racist overtones of his doctrine, and most important, to play a profound influence in the development of the black man's militant stance.

On April 3, 1964, less than one month after leaving the Nation of Islam, Malcolm X addressed a predominantly black audience in Cleveland at a symposium sponsored by the local chapter of the Congress of Racial Equality on the topic "The Negro Revolt—What Comes Next?". In view of the revolution taking place in his own life at that time the topic was a profoundly personal one. His approach centered on the two major problems which he faced, consisting of the necessity to redefine his position in the Negro community, and to articulate modifications in his vision for that community's plan of action. This was certainly no simple task. Eldridge Cleaver provides a graphic description:

> . . . These events caused a profound personal crisis in my life and beliefs, as it did for other Muslims. During the bitter time of his suspension and prior to his break with Elijah Muhammad, we had watched Malcolm X as he sought frantically to reorient himself and establish a new platform. It was like watching a master do a dance with death on a highstrung tightrope. He pirouetted, twirled, turned somersaults in the air—but he landed firmly on his feet and was off and running.[2]

It was a task begun shortly before the actual break, and one demanding immediate action. The April 3 speech, although it does not represent the

Peggy Reynolds is a graduate student and teaching associate in the Department of Speech, Communication and Theatre Arts at the University of Minnesota.

[1] James Baldwin, *The Fire Next Time* (New York: Dell, c. 1962).
[2] Eldridge Cleaver, *Soul on Ice* (New York: Dell, 1968), p. 54.

maturity of Malcolm's later thoughts, is a succinct statement of both aspects
of the problem of reestablishing his leadership. Likewise, the content, which
is representative of a common theme in his oratory, has enjoyed extended
influence, and is remarkably congruent with the later formulations of 'Black
Power' advocates.

The speech which Malcolm presented was entitled "The Ballot or the
Bullet," and he forthrightly disposed of the leadership question in the first
five minutes. The title introduced the essence of his discourse. Before ex-
panding on his topic he hastened to assuage his audience's curiosity by
establishing "I'm still a Muslim."[3] This simple summation of the extended
trauma he had undergone in his break with Elijah Muhammad provides one
example of how he turned circumstances to his advantage. For, in spite of
the history of sectarian differences and his own ostracized position from the
Muslim fold, he used it to align himself with and attempt to unify his
audience:

> . . . I'm not here to try and change your religion. I'm not here to argue or
> discuss anything that we differ about, because it's time for us to submerge
> our differences and realize that it is best for us to first see that we have the
> same problem, a common problem—a problem that will make you catch
> hell whether you're a Baptist, or a Methodist, or a Muslim, or a nationalist.
> . . . We're all in the same boat and we all are going to catch the same
> hell from the same man. He just happens to be the white man.[4]

The audience to which Malcolm X directed this speech, both immediate and
extended, was essentially a *black* audience. And in spite of the fact that he
was a 'fallen' leader, that he was proposing a highly unorthodox strategy
from the platform of an erstwhile 'liberal' non-violent organization (CORE),
that he was attempting to spark an issue held in rein by contemporary token
legislation, and that he was trying to crystallize a *raison d'etre* in the fact of
personal upheaval—he was able to grasp the one overriding common feature
which he held with his audience, their blackness, and rather powerfully suggest that it was the most valid frame of reference from which to begin.

The ensuing expansion on his theme is a compendium of forms of proof,
but relies heavily on the value of *ethos*. The style, delivery and organization
are variations on the theme. For this is Malcolm X speaking, and as already
suggested, that is the central determinant for the speech's effectiveness.

Stylistically, Malcolm's speeches tend to be conversational, and the format
of "The Ballot or the Bullet" is only superficially more formal. A typical introduction might read, "We want to have just an off-the-cuff chat between
you and me, us."[5] In this speech, however, probably partly as a function of
the occasion and partly tongue-in-cheek, Malcolm begins by formally addressing his audience, and quickly lapses into a more conversational tone: "Mr.
Moderator . . . , friends and enemies: I just can't believe that everyone in
here is a friend and don't want to leave anybody out."[6] He not only is, but
speaks like one of his audience.

The bulk of the speech is a clarification of one central idea—the impor-

---

[3] Malcolm X, "The Ballot or the Bullet," delivered in Cleveland on April 3, 1964,
reprinted in *Malcolm X Speaks,* ed. George Breitman (New York: Grove Press,
1965), p. 24.

[4] *Ibid.*

[5] Malcolm X, "Message to the Grass Roots," reprinted in *Malcolm X Speaks,* p. 4.

[6] Malcolm X, "The Ballot or the Bullet," *loc. cit.*

tance of a stable socio-economic self-made community, via *whatever* means—
the ballot or the bullet—nonviolent "channels" or violence. The devices consistently employed are repetition and analogy. The catch-phrase ("Ballot or
the Bullet") is repeated, for example, approximately fourteen times (not
counting allusions to it). Figurative analogy appears to be another favorite,
such as:

> I'm not going to sit at your table and watch you eat, with nothing on my
> plate, and call myself a diner. Sitting at the table doesn't make you a diner
> unless you eat some of what's on that plate. Being here doesn't make you
> American.[7]

Likewise, in keeping with the "conversation" with "just people" approach,
Malcolm's vocabulary is very simple. He capitalizes on this:

> You know what is meant by "reciprocal"? That's one of Brother Lomax's
> words, I stole it from him. I don't usually deal with these big words
> because I usually don't deal with big people. I deal with small people.[8]

Taken together, these stylistic elements serve to augment the thesis. Like
many of the dynamic spokesmen for Black Power who followed (cf. Carmichael, Cleaver . . .), the style adapted in addressing the black community
has been carefully geared to avoid flowery pretentiousness in preference for
the simple and graphic oratory of 'telling-it-like-it-is.'

In terms of content, the direction which he takes to clarify the theme
elicits assumptions quite analogous to those presented later by Carmichael
and Hamilton in their now classic attempt to clarify the meaning of Black
Power. The fundamental cry has been for the self-determinism of the community. Both Malcolm X and the Carmichael and Hamilton duo, much as
prophets in the wilderness, are wary of the subtle bonds which prevent its
realization. Carmichael and Hamilton explicitly refer to these barriers as the
"Myths of Coalition,"[9] which may be summarized as awareness of an underlying support of "Anglo-conformity" in the "white liberal" camp which espouses
its love for its "black brethren," the power base of political and economic
security irrevocably located in the "white" camp, and the fallacy that "white
liberal" intervention is conscience-based. In the CORE address Malcolm X
mercilessly hammers at each of these. To the point of a fundamentally
WASP-based society he declares:

> . . . . The same government . . . is in a conspiracy to deprive you of your
> voting rights, . . . of economic opportunities, . . . of decent housing, . . . of
> decent education. . . . it is the government itself which is responsible for
> the oppression and exploitation and degradation of black people in this
> country.[10]

Regarding the socio-economic power-structure he says, "The economic
philosophy of black nationalism is pure and simple. It only means that we
should control the economy of our community."[11] And to the question of a
"conscience motivation" he declares:

---

[7] *Ibid.*, p. 26
[8] *Ibid.*, p. 32.
[9] Stokely Carmichael and Charles V. Hamilton, *Black Power* (New York: Random House, 1967), pp. 58–84.
[10] Malcolm X, "The Ballot or the Bullet," *op. cit.*, p. 31.
[11] *Ibid.*, p. 38.

Don't change the white man's mind—you can't change his mind and that
whole thing about appealing to the moral conscience of America—America's conscience is bankrupt . . . We have to change our own mind.[12]

Stylistically and thematically such presentations as this bridge the gap
between the quiet passivity and cooperative tactics of such figures as Booker
T. Washington and Dr. Martin Luther King and the vociferous emergence
of a rhetorical manifestation of a new kind of "pride." And in a wider spectrum, Malcolm's own biography, as one small element in the midst of large-
scale turmoil, is somewhat analogous to the black man's cyclic repression and
release. Black history is replete with cyclic repression—most dramatically
represented in the move from the institution of slavery to emancipation—but
to be repeated in the slow struggle from the economic enslavement of the
ghetto towards civil rights through superficial legislative promises. Malcolm
X moved from slavish devotion to the Harlem underground, to a succession of
prisons, to unquestioning adherence to Elijah Muhammad's Nation of Islam,
to the "emancipated" status from which this speech emerges (which might
even yet be seen as servitude to a later modified ideology). There is likewise
a movement from a religiously based "faith" or resignation in the face of the
inevitable to a secular concern with the efficacy of group endeavor.

Much as Malcolm X's background and rhetorical strategies produce a unique
and productive approach to long-standing ills, the hue and cry of Black
Power, born of its own brand of turmoil, demands a drastically different plan
of action. Malcolm reiterates: "When you're under someone else's control,
you're segregated . . . You've got to *control* your own. Just like the white man
. . ."[13] The keynote is neither over-intellectualization nor pseudo-cooperation
but long overdue straightforward self-determination. In no uncertain terms
we find that ". . . it is time . . . if you are a man, to let that man know."[14]

---

[12] *Ibid.*, p. 40.
[13] *Ibid.*, p. 42.
[14] *Ibid.*, p. 43.

ON NIXON'S KENNEDY STYLE

RONALD H. CARPENTER AND ROBERT V. SELTZER

Style is personal. A man's unique lexical and syntactical choices are reflective of his singular condition. Exigencies of audience and situation may determine the arguments and appeals used in discourse, but as stated in Buffon's celebrated epigram, "The style is the man himself."[1] It seems incongruous that a man of Richard M. Nixon's background and temperament should assume the very personal and different style in discourse of a man of John F. Kennedy's significantly divergent background and temperament. In *The Making of the President 1968*, however, Theodore White reported that phenomenon, hearing in Richard M. Nixon's speaking "the echo of the phrases of John F. Kennedy in 1960."[2] Here, we compare the famous Kennedy Inaugural Address of 1960 with Nixon's crucial Acceptance Address at the 1968 Republican National Convention to illustrate two major stylistic sources of that echo.[3]

First, recall the salient elements of the John F. Kennedy style in discourse. In his brief years of national prominence, the former President established a personal, highly identifiable style. It is immaterial whether any given turn of phrase came from Theodore Sorensen or other writers. The crucial point is that certain stylistic forms characterized John F. Kennedy's Inaugural Address and other public discourse to become intimately associated with the man himself. Foremost among these usages are parallel repetitions and the almost ubiquitous antitheses.

Antithesis evolves when utterance elements of contrasting meanings are arranged syntactically to be contiguous or in close proximity. Although rhetoricians identify six variations of antithetical form, the usage involves basically apposition of antonyms or clauses with opposing semantic content. John F. Kennedy's Inaugural Address contains some twenty-eight antitheses. Antonyms in proximity to one another appear, for instance, in "*support* any *friend* or *oppose* any *foe*" or in the antithesis between "the *many* who are *poor*" and "the *few* who are *rich*." Or note the antithesis between "*United*, there is little we *cannot* do. . . . *Divided*, there is little we *can* do." Apposition of clauses with opposing semantic content is illustrated by the familiar "*Ask not what your country can do for you—Ask what you can do for your country.*"

Parallel repetition results from beginning or concluding successive phrases, short sentences, or very brief paragraphs with the same word or words. The Kennedy Inaugural also utilized this structure often, as in "*To those* old

---

Mr. Carpenter is Assistant Professor of Speech at Wayne State University; Mr. Seltzer is Instructor and Director of Forensics at the University of Detroit.

[1] Buffon, "Address on Style," in *The Art of the Writer,* ed. Lane Cooper (Ithaca: Cornell University Press, 1952), p. 153.

[2] Theodore H. White, *The Making of the President 1968* (New York: Atheneum Press, 1969), p. 131.

[3] The text of the Kennedy address is that provided by Ernest J. Wrage and Barnet Baskerville in *Contemporary Forum: American Speeches on Twentieth-Century Issues* (New York: Harper and Brothers, 1962), p. 317; the text of the Nixon speech is that appearing in *U.S. News and World Report* (August 19, 1968), 54.

allies. . . . *To those* new states. . . . *To those* people in the huts and villages.
. . ." The following entreaty, for example, also is characterized by parallel repetition.

> *Let both sides* explore what problems unite us instead of belaboring
> those problems which divide us.
> *Let both sides*, for the first time, formulate serious and precise proposals
> for the inspection and control of arms—and bring the absolute power to
> destroy other nations under the absolute control of all nations.
> *Let both sides* seek to invoke the wonders of science instead of its terrors.

And even within this parallelism are the antitheses between *unite* and *divide*,
absolute power and *absolute control*, or *wonders* of science instead of its
terrors.

Prior to 1968, Richard M. Nixon's extensive use of the extemporaneous
mode of delivery allowed ample rehearsal of and reliance upon such stock
phrases as: "I want to make it perfectly clear what I mean"; "I have been
asked why I do this and this is my answer"; and "What do I mean by 'freedom?' This is what I mean by 'freedom.' " His characteristic style in discourse, however, did not include to a noticeable extent John F. Kennedy's
stylistic tendencies.

In 1968 there was a change. At times during the campaign and particularly
in the Acceptance Address to the Republican Convention, the attempt to project the image of a "New Nixon" saw some unique additions to well rehearsed
stylistic habits. These alterations were described by White only as an "echo"
of John F. Kennedy; it may be more appropriate here to ruminate about
these additions as attempts to use a style highly reminiscent of the man who
won the Presidency in 1960. For momentarily, a New Nixon was Old Kennedy.

Stylistic maneuvers such as antitheses are not typical of the customary and
familiar idiom; and as marked deviations from idiomatic usage, these usages
often require conscientious effort to construct.[4] Richard M. Nixon exerted
that kind of personal effort in preparing his Acceptance Address before the
Republican National Convention. Although the future President often relied
extensively upon his writers, William H. Honan notes that this speech was an
exception.

> In another instance, however—the acceptance speech at the convention—
> Nixon wrote the text himself. He had idea conferences with several of his
> writers and all of them submitted drafts or at least cheer lines—some of
> which he used; but Nixon put it together and wrote it out—first in outline
> form on a legal-sized yellow tablet, and then draft after draft by dicta-
> phone.[5]

The syntax and lexicon of this speech are personal to the President-to-be.

But Richard M. Nixon's so personally prepared Acceptance Address of
1968 is studded with the stylistic conformations associated more readily with
John F. Kennedy. The speech uses some forty antitheses! Note for instance

---

[4] For a discussion and compilation of all the traditionally recommended depar-
tures from syntactical norms, see Ronald H. Carpenter, "The Essential Schemes of
Syntax: An Analysis of Rhetorical Theory's Recommendations for Uncommon
Word Orders," *Quarterly Journal of Speech* (April 1969), 161–168.

[5] William H. Honan, "The Men Behind Nixon's Speeches," *New York Times
Magazine* (January 19, 1969), 65.

the antithetical "After an *era of confrontation* the time has come for an *era of negotiation*" or the more overt antithesis between "We shall *always* negotiate from *strength* and *never* from *weakness*." (Perhaps this is an "echo" in form and content of Kennedy's "Let us never *negotiate out of fear*. But let us never *fear to negotiate*.") The conformation also is utilized in statements such as "Let us accept this challenge, not as a *grim duty*, but as an *exciting adventure*" and a very Kennedyesque "If we are to have *respect for law* in America we must have *laws that deserve respect*."

Parallel repetitions are used some thirty times. For example, the future President spoke of those failures "*when the* strongest nation in the world can be tied down for four years in a war in Vietnam with no end in sight, *when the* richest nation in the world can't manage its own economy, *when the* nation with the richest tradition of the rule of law is plagued by unprecedented lawlessness. . . ." (Should we suggest the antithesis between *rule of law* and *unprecedented lawlessness*?) The same phrase, "I see a day," began seven successive brief paragraphs. This usage was inspired, according to Honan, by a memorandum from speech writer William Safire who recommended the device as typical of other famous speakers, including Franklin D. Roosevelt, Adlai E. Stevenson, Martin Luther King and—John F. Kennedy.[6]

Why emulate a Kennedy style in discourse? Some speculation may be in order. Theodore White might attribute the emulation to a belief that "no human contact ever takes place without leaving some permanent mark. . . . The mark of John F. Kennedy was seared into Richard M. Nixon in 1960. . . ."[7] There is, however, at least one other possible explanation. Imitation well may be a means of identification. Richard M. Nixon admits to using this tactic before when the 1952 Fund Speech referred to his dog Checkers in conscious imitation of Franklin D. Roosevelt's "devastating" reference to his dog Fala in the campaign of 1944.[8] A possible effect of stylistic imitation would be to create an "echo" and perhaps—if style *is* the man—even evince some substance of John F. Kennedy and thus gain a measure of the admiration and support attained by the winner of 1960.

Whether or not this could be the case is really beyond the scope of this commentary. The noteworthy point here is the apparently conscientious effort exerted by one man to depart from his customary stylistic tendencies to use for an important occasion a different style so intimately associated with another man. And what could be more noteworthy language behavior than a Richard M. Nixon using a John F. Kennedy style?

---

[6] *Ibid.*

[7] White, *loc. cit.*

[8] Richard M. Nixon, *Six Crises* (New York: Doubleday and Company, 1962), p. 103.

THE RHETORIC OF ALIGNMENT: CAN NIXON'S QUEST FOR POWER UNITE THE NATION?

JAMES W. CHESEBRO AND SANDRA E. PURNELL

During the 1968 Presidential campaign, Richard Nixon said he possessed a "plan" to reduce America's involvement in Vietnam. Because of diplomatic and military considerations, Nixon argued that the details of the "plan" could not then be released. After nine months in office and after a major Vietnam moratorium, people were even more anxious to know how and when the conflict would be resolved. In October, Nixon committed himself to a November 3rd policy statement on Vietnam. For three weeks, expectations rose and predictions regarding the speech were made with increasing frequency. The address was perceived as a significant statement for both the nation's survival and Nixon's political success. Because of the political significance of this address, then, a rhetorical analysis is appropriate.[1]

Rhetorically, the November 3rd speech has three major structural divisions. In the first third of the speech, the President provides a history of the war. Strategically, Nixon identifies the war with the last three administrations and argues that the war represents an emerging and developing policy—a policy not to be dismissed hastily. This section subtly merges into the second third of the speech by way of a discussion of the negotiations in Paris and other secret negotiations. In the second section of the speech, Nixon outlines his proposal for ending the war, including a summary of his correspondence with Ho Chi Minh and of the process of Vietnamization of the war. The final section of the speech seems to be an attempt to control and direct the reactions of the audience. He recaptures a great American "national destiny" for the "great silent majority" and apparently seeks to reduce the antagonism of the "vocal minority." After identifying this three-part division in the speech, a critic might terminate his descriptive analysis. However, this division provides the foundation for an examination of how Nixon was able to use such a descriptive analysis for significant, yet unstated, persuasive purposes.

As a result, we shall focus upon the November 3rd speech in terms of its purposes. We shall ask: (1) What purposes are overtly stated in the speech? (2) What are the unstated but actual or operational persuasive purposes of the speech? (3) How effective was Nixon's rhetorical effort? An examination of the transcript reveals two apparent purposes for delivering this speech. First, Nixon sought to increase unity in the nation and reduce the degree and significance of dissent. Second, he wanted to improve his own political power base or position by uniting the majority of the nation behind the Nixon plan. Initially, these two goals are theoretically

---

James W. Chesebro (M.S., Illinois State University, 1967) and Sandra Purnell (M.A., Wayne State University, 1966) are Ph.D. Candidates and Teaching Associates in the Department of Speech, Communication, and Theatre Arts, University of Minnesota, Minneapolis, Minnesota.

[1] All quotations are from the Nixon speech as completely reported in the *Minneapolis Tribune*, November 4, 1969.

compatible. Perhaps the best way to reduce dissent would be to unite the conflicting groups behind a universally appealing Nixon program. The question this article will attempt to answer is whether Nixon was able to achieve both objectives. The major thesis developed here is that Nixon successfully achieved a renewed and powerful political base, but failed to unite the nation.

RECAPTURING THE POWER BASE

The "great silent majority" represents the essential power that Nixon must possess to sustain viable political control. The upper and middle class whites provided the financial support for Nixon's campaign, provided the ballots for his election, and appear to be the only group capable of sustaining his national prestige. Nixon must sustain the confidence of this majority.

However, the Vietnam issue threatened the security of this majority. The strong and active support of this group began to "splinter" into fractions. The Vietnam war had reinforced perplexing problems for this group and thus threatened Nixon's political power base. How did this occur? The universality and significance of the war brought all disparate elements and minority values to the foreground, constituting a direct threat to the majority. Youth had again been pitted against the "older generation." The wild-eyed hippie and yippie, automatically a threat to traditional values, appeared to be successfully undermining respect for the President, the national prestige and the "free world." Withdrawing from Vietnam also carried the connotations that America will lose a war, that young people will not fight for their nation, that Communism should be allowed to grow and subjugate the weak nations of the world. These were the issues and the rhetorical problem Nixon had to address in his November 3rd speech. Nixon did, in fact, effectively respond to this situation as defined by the majority. Rhetorically the situation required that Nixon employ two major families of rhetoric—*a rhetoric of placement* and *a rhetoric of power*.

A rhetoric of placement requires that strategies be employed which define and defend a believable view of world events—an acceptable reality. Rhetorically, a speaker may define reality in many ways. For instance, he may divide the world into friendly and unfriendly forces as he sees them or as he wishes to see them. Nixon was forced to define reality in such a fashion that his Vietnam proposal appeared to be an effective response to the war and yet allowed the majority again to be united in their perception of reality.

The rhetoric of power is a major family of terms that provides the basis for effective assertion—the potential of action behind the word. Kenneth Burke argues that several kinds of strategies might be selected from this family- and, in list form, these strategies might be one or more of the following:

> . . .social power, sexual, physical, political, military, commercial, mone-
> tary, mental, moral, stylistic (powers of grace, grandeur, vituperation,
> precision)—powers of emancipation, liberalization, separation ("loos-
> ing"), powers of fascination and fascization ("binding," as in Mann's
> "Mario and the Magician")—and powers of wisdom, understanding,
> knowledge.[2]

---

[2] Kenneth Burke, *The Philosophy of Literary Form* (Vintage Books of Random House, New York, 1957), x.

A rhetoric of power was needed by Nixon. A rhetoric of power would provide a set of strategies to guarantee the security and control desired by the majority.

Initially, then, the rhetoric of placement, for Nixon, involved a redefinition of the circumstances and events involved in the war. By choice, reality is redefined or created in the traditional language and values of the majority. For Nixon, however, this placement strategy might be aptly entitled, "the celebration of a lost heritage." In essence this strategy assumed that the audience felt a powerful commitment to an active and strong form of American leadership in international affairs. This pride leads easily to the rhetorical assertion that America should act—act to control and eliminate evil in the world. Nixon defines the major question of Vietnam in terms of America's role or place in international affairs. He states:

> Let us all understand that the question before us is not whether some Americans are for peace and some against it. The great question at issue is not whether Johnson's war becomes Nixon's war. The question is: how can we win America's peace?

For some observers, the rhetorical question might have been "how can peace be achieved in the world?" For Nixon, however, the question implies that America must *win* the war, and that *America's peace,* not world peace, is the issue. The traditional role of America in international affairs is reasserted. The language and world view of this celebration of a lost heritage allowed the majority to identify in a potent and united fashion. Why? Clearly, the traditional values of the "older generation" were reasserted as viable and significant. National prestige, a "free world," the use of war as a tool of international relations, and the casting of Communism as the enemy to be fought—all of these values and perspectives of the 1950's are reasserted to appease generations of the '50's.

Moreover, the first third of the speech, although some might call it a historical description, functions to redefine reality with America as the central focus of power and control. This description of America persuasively reasserts the traditional values and perspectives of the older, silent majority. The basis for unity is again provided. In this first third of the speech, Nixon phrases his first question of concern as a question of fact, "Why and how did the United States become involved in Vietnam in the first place?" Note, however, that such a description would involve choices— not all data can be presented, and the data selected must also allow Nixon to argue that his proposal ultimately is responsive to the Vietnam situation. Thus, the first third of the speech is more aptly perceived as a strategy, not a historical description. This "historical" strategy functions ultimately to define America as a force of good fighting the Communistic forces of evil. Thus, Nixon describes the initial inception of the war:

> Fifteen years ago North Vietnam, with the logistic support of Communist China and the Soviet Union, launched a campaign to impose a Communist government on South Vietnam by instigating and supporting a revolution.

The effort of all three Presidents before him, argues Nixon, was to "prevent a Communist takeover." For Nixon, the problem remains much the same— the United States must pit itself against the forces of Communism: "Our precipitate withdrawal would inevitably allow the Communists to repeat the massacres which followed their takeover of the North fifteen years ago," with the "atrocities of Hue" becoming the "nightmare of the entire nation," and "For the United States, this first defeat in our nation's history would result in a collapse of confidence in American leadership, not only in Asia but throughout the world." Thus, Nixon would reassert a foreign policy which gives the United States a major role as an acting, not reacting, agent:

> For the future of peace, precipitate withdrawal would thus be a disaster of immense magnitude. —A Nation cannot remain great if it betrays its allies and lets down its friends. —Our defeat and humiliation in South Vietnam would without question promote recklessness in the councils of those great powers who have not yet abandoned their goals of world conquest. —This would spark violence wherever our commitments help maintain peace—in the Middle East, in Berlin, eventually even in the Western Hemisphere.

For the great majority, Nixon, then, offers a celebration of a lost heritage. Overtly, Nixon notes:

> I know it may not be fashionable to speak of patriotism or national destiny these days. But I feel it is appropriate to do so on this occasion. Two hundred years ago this nation was weak and poor. But even then, America was the hope of millions in the world. Today we have become the strongest and richest nation in the world. The wheel of destiny has turned so that any hope the world has for survival of peace and freedom in the last third of this century will be determined by whether the American people have the moral stamina and courage to meet the challenge of free world leadership.

The heritage, once lost, shall be regained and the United States shall once again become the active and controlling agent in world affairs. This strategic "celebration of a lost heritage" leads easily to Nixon's second major strategy.

Nixon moves, in the second and third sections of the speech, through a proposal and assessment of the proposal on his audience. Specifically, the second section of the speech—the Nixon proposal—is acceptable because the situation is defined in terms that allow Nixon the right slowly to withdraw troops, given the objectives of America and the nature of Communism as the enemy. In the third section of the speech, there is an apparent appeal for unity. Clearly, the majority is provided with security. The minority, however, becomes a scapegoat for the guarantee provided to the majority. A rhetorical analysis seems to support this view of the two last parts of the speech. While the rhetoric of placement and the strategy of celebrating a lost heritage provides a partial basis for this analysis, one must also identify Nixon's second major family of rhetoric. The rhetoric of power and Nixon's specific strategy are complementary to his first strategy, yet also provide credibility to the Nixon proposal and a basis for our suggestion that the minority is the sacrificial lamb employed to secure the support of the Nixon proposal by the majority.

Given that America should define itself as an active and powerful force in world affairs, Nixon is ready to become the means or powerful force necessary to achieve that placement for America. For Nixon, the rhetoric of power becomes a strategy of "leadership—a personal assertion." The emphasis shifts from a concern for what Nixon might propose ("I have not and do not intend to announce the timetable of our program.") to faith in Nixon as an effective and decisive leader. Nixon would identify American foreign policy with his personal decisions. Indeed, the plan is a "Nixon plan." Underscoring his personal commitment to leadership, Nixon states:

> I recognized that a long and bitter war like this usually cannot be settled in a public forum. That is why in addition to the public statements and negotiations, I have explored every possible private avenue that might lead to a settlement. . .I did not wait for my inauguration to begin my quest for peace.

Later, regarding the Nixon plan:

> If I conclude that increased enemy action jeopardizes our remaining forces in Vietnam, I shall not hesitate to take strong and effective measures to deal with that situation.

Power and leadership shall reside in Nixon himself. The majority is given confidence—a strong and dynamic leader is promised to ensure that the majority shall rule. Nixon will become the "figurehead of America" and assume the "burden" of a "first defeat" if that occurs. Philosophically, Nixon has made a renewed commitment to *idealism*—the world experiences and values of a man, Nixon, will become the basis for action in international affairs. While clearly responsive to the great silent majority, such a philosophical choice does exclude other philosophical positions. *Materialism,* the nature of circumstances and events around men, shall not be the basis for action. However, the rhetoric of placement and power do become the basis for strategies that do recapture the power base for Nixon. The "celebration of a lost heritage" and "leadership" as "a personal assertion" redefined reality and provided both the means and end desired by the great silent majority. However, for the vocal minority, the November 3rd speech apparently rejects the significance of dissent.

ALIENATION OF THE VOCAL MINORITY

The vocal minority sees Nixon as rejecting their philosophical orientation, their view of reality, and their view of meaningful dissent in a democracy. These three fundamental differences ensure that the minority will not be drawn into the Nixon coalition. For the minority, Nixon elicits a response of silent disgust and sets the stage for permanent division in America.

In this speech, Nixon promises to recapture a lost heritage. Because the American people are an active, "do-it-yourself" people, likewise American foreign policy might again *act*—direct and control international affairs. Clearly, such a position directly counters the volumes of material that define the philosophical orientation of the minority.[3] The minority sees America's

---

[3] The concept of the *vocal minority* may be an effective rhetorical choice; however; it is extremely difficult to determine who Nixon is referring to by his use of this term. In identifying what we believe to be the *vocal minority,* our analysis of the philosophy, world-view and self-image of the vocal minority has been guided by two major groupings of writers and speakers. One group, essentially liberals, include Eugene McCarthy (*The Limits of Power, America's Role in the World,* Dell Publishing Co., Inc., New York, 1968), J. William Fulbright (especially *The Vietnam Hearings,* Random House, New York, 1966), Robert F. Kennedy (*A New Day,* The New American Library, New York, 1968, and *To Seek a Newer World,* Garden City, 1967), and Franz Schurmann, Peter Dale Scott, and Reginald Zelnik (*The Politics of Escalation in Vietnam,* Fawcett World Library, New York, 1966). The other group of speakers and writers, essentially radicals, used to determine the orientation of the vocal minority rests upon the

role as essentially one of *reacting* to world events. The United States should react to, not attempt to establish, the relationships among other nation-states, and should sustain only a supportive military role. Specifically, then, regarding Vietnam, protestors argue that the United States, as a third party to a civil war, is not and should not be in a position of power in Vietnam. Moreover, the United States should play a secondary role, it is noted, because Vietnam is not in the self-interest of the United States and the outcome of the war cannot be controlled. It is also noted by the minority that a commitment to a third-world revolution and anti-colonialism requires that America react to the needs of the third-world nations, remaining in a supportive position if involved at all. This philosophical orientation of the minority strongly conflicts with Nixon's action orientation and would make the speech unacceptable to the radical. These philosophical differences are reflected in a second major area of disagreement—the nature of reality.

The radical's view of reality directly conflicts with Nixon's view of the history of the Vietnam war in the first third of his speech. Several apparent conflicts exist. The conflicts cannot be developed here but their nature can be identified.

1. Nixon suggests that this is a traditional war of aggression: "Fifteen years ago North Vietnam. . .launched a campaign to impose a Communist government on South Vietnam by instigating and supporting a revolution." The dissenter would argue that the war was originally a civil war among indigenous elements of the Vietnamese people. Ho Chi Minh was motivated by nationalism and a desire for independence from both France and Red China.

2. Nixon suggests that there has been a single policy on Vietnam carried out by four Presidents: "Three American Presidents have recognized the great stakes involved in Vietnam and understood what had to be done." Opponents of the war have constantly observed that Eisenhower was extremely wary of a land war in Asia and provided only support for the French Army, not American troops. Kennedy, although he spoke of defending the *independence* of South Vietnam (not necessarily against an independent *Communist* state), sent Americans only in an advisory role as part of an economic program. It is apparent that military assistance is quite different from the commitment of 500,000 American troops.

3. Nixon suggests that immediate withdrawal would result in a collapse of confidence in American leadership. Opponents have argued that our involvement has already cost us the confidence and respect of many allies and awakened fears among the other small third-world nations.

4. Nixon suggests that Vietnam is vital to the national self-interests of the United States. The assumption has been questioned: How can so small and poor a nation be significant to the United States? Vietnam, it has been proposed, might be strategically most effective as an independent, perhaps Communist, buffer state between our Pacific allies and Communist China.

---

works of Kenneth Keniston (*Young Radicals, Notes on Committed Youths,* Harcourt, Brace and World, Inc., New York, 1968), Paul Jacobs and Saul Landau (*The New Radicals: A Report with Documents,* Random House, New York, 1966), Christopher Lasch (*The New Radicalism In America 1889–1963,* Random House, New York, 1965), Irving Howe (*The Radical Papers,* Anchor Books, New York, 1966), and Jack Newfield (*A Prophetic Minority,* The New American Library, New York, 1966).

5. The President suggests that failure in Vietnam would result in further wars "in the Middle East, in Berlin and eventually even in the Western Hemisphere." This appears to be an indirect expression of the fear of wars of national liberation directed by Moscow or Peking. This fear rests on the assumption that there is an aggressive, monolithic Communist conspiracy, an assumption which has been shaken by the Sino-Soviet split and by the relative failure of attempts to export revolution in Africa and South America. The dissenter would reject the emphasis Nixon places upon the "great powers who have not yet abandoned their goals of world conquest."

6. Finally, the dissenter would probably disagree with Nixon's interpretation of the Paris negotiations. Nixon implies that he is waiting for the enemy to capitulate, while the dissenter might be more interested in seeing the United States make more major concessions. This is further exemplified in Nixon's definition of the nature of Ho Chi Minh's letter. Nixon implies that the letter is merely a restatement of North Vietnam's hard-line position on a settlement. The tone of the letter, however, and the fact that it was a direct response to Nixon outside of normal diplomatic channels suggests a slight softening of attitude in the North.

Thus it appears likely that the Vietnam war dissenter would disagree almost completely with the first section of Nixon's speech and, as a result, disagree with the basis for the second part of the speech, the Nixon plan. Nixon's view of reality appears diametrically opposed to the interpretation of reality offered by war opponents. This second area of disagreement upon the nature of reality becomes even more significant when the image of the dissenter is discussed by Nixon. Nixon's image of the dissenter appears to differ from the dissenter's self-image on two counts: (1) the political position of the dissenter and (2) the impact of dissent on American foreign policy.

First, Nixon equates the dissenter's political position with "taking the easy way out" and losing the war. He suggests that there are only two options—complete withdrawal or Vietnamization of the war. Nixon states:

I have chosen the second course.
It is not the easy way.
It is the right way.

Thus, the President sets up a dichotomy, putting himself on the side of "rightness" and the dissenters on the side of "easiness." This is not a flattering interpretation of the dissenter's political position. But moreover, the fact that Nixon seems ready to make such a dichotomy in the first place—the dissenter and Nixon occupy different political positions—reminds one of Carmichael's analysis of LBJ: "Johnson drew the color lines." Perhaps the dissenter would say, "Nixon drew the battle lines."

Having defined the political position of the dissenter, Nixon suggests the impact that these young people are attempting to exert:

. . .as President of the United States, I would be untrue to my oath of office if I allowed the policy of this nation to be dictated by the minority who hold that view and who attempt to impose it on the nation by mounting demonstrations in the street.

Later, Nixon argues, "If a vocal minority, however fervent its causes, prevails over reason and the will of the majority this nation has no future as a free society." Thus, the demonstrators, rather than contributing to democratic decision-making by exhibiting support for one side of the issue via the constitutional right to petition the government, are attempting to dictate policy and circumvent reason. In the radical's view, demonstrators certainly do not expect to dictate government policy. Most seem to bemoan their apparent lack of influence in high councils. Nixon's statement must be counted as either entirely unreasonable or as an indication that he feels threatened, overpowered by the demonstrators.

As a form of summarizing position, the total impact of the minority is dealt a final blow by Nixon when he states: "I respect your idealism." When the entire tenor of the speech suggests that everything the dissenter believes is either wrong or unpatriotic, it is not credible that the President could respect their "idealism" except in a very peculiar and perhaps insulting way. The statement in this context seems to imply a kind of youthful, starry-eyed and quite foolish idealism. Certainly the dissenters do not view themselves as so incredibly naive.

Thus this speech was incapable of winning the support or even indulgence of the antiwar demonstrators. Though Nixon mentioned the desire to draw the people together and listen to every group, this speech seems almost designed to alienate the already disenchanted youth of the United States. Nixon's rehearsal of the events of the war would outrage many. If that did not, the discussion of the unpatriotic, undemocratic demonstrator in the street no doubt would result in outrage. Operationally Nixon may have in this speech received political support from the majority by using the minority as a scapegoat or sacrifical lamb to gain the laurels of the majority.[4]

CONCLUSION

Focusing upon the purposes of Nixon's November 3rd speech, we have suggested that the descriptive emphasis of the speech should not prevent us from recognizing Nixon's strong persuasive effort. The first third of the speech, while cast as a historical description, nonetheless is a persuasive attempt to redefine reality. The second part of the speech, while cast as a description of the Nixon plan, nonetheless is a persuasive attempt to unify the majority. The third part of the speech, while cast as an appeal to national unity, nonetheless is a persuasive attempt to use the minority as a scapegoat to guarantee the security of the majority. Thus, Nixon's rhetorical effort is persuasive, and the question we have asked is whether Nixon could recapture his political power and also unite the nation. Employing the strategies that would celebrate a lost heritage with a commitment to a personal assertion of leadership, Nixon did, we have argued, regain his political power base provided by the great silent majority. For the vocal minority, however, different philosophical orientations, views of reality, and the image of the dissenter permanently separated Nixon and the dissenter, thus dividing, not uniting, the nation. From an even larger perspective, however, a critic might argue that Nixon denies the role of dissent in a democracy and minimizes the significance of free communication. Thus, major ethical questions may emerge regarding Nixon as a public speaker.

---

[4] The rhetoric and proposals of Spiro Agnew might be perceived as an extension of Nixon's use of the minority in this fashion. If this is the case, Nixon is overtly aware of his use of the minority. Such an analysis might provide the foundation for an ethical judgment of Nixon.

SPIRO AGNEW'S DIVERSIONARY RHETORIC

BERNARD L. BROCK

Spiro T. Agnew has again become an outspoken, controversial political figure. During the Presidential campaign Mr. Agnew gained a reputation for "shooting from the hip" which caused many people to question his qualifications as a Vice President, much less as a possible President. But during the 10 months following the election he was a different man—he quietly slipped into the background. However, this month with a series of speeches in which he attacked the moratorium peace leaders and the TV and press news media, Mr. Agnew has returned to the limelight, reinforcing his previous "reckless" image.

After successfully assuming a subordinate role and gaining a great deal of favorable comment because of this role change, one must question *why* Mr. Agnew suddenly reverted to a role which most observers would agree reduces his chances ever to be a Presidential candidate for his party. Was this a sudden whim which seized him, or is this role change part of a broader strategy within the Nixon administration? In considering the timing of his recent speeches and the effects that they've had on Mr. Nixon's major problem, Vietnam, the conclusion that Mr. Agnew's speeches are a co-ordinate part of Mr. Nixon's Vietnam effort is hard to reject. In fact, it appears as if Mr. Agnew is presently engaged in diversionary rhetoric.

Having previously attacked the leaders of the peace movement, on October 30th Mr. Agnew made a formal speech in which he took a stand on Vietnam: "Chanting 'Peace Now' is no solution, if 'Peace Now' is to permit wholesale Bloodbath." Then after Mr. Agnew's position received reasonable public acceptance, on November 3rd Mr. Nixon in a nation-wide TV address on Vietnam took a similar stand. It now appears as if Mr. Agnew's October 30th speech was a trial balloon which allowed Mr. Nixon to make his Vietnam policy more vague and to move toward the political right.

Following his address Mr. Nixon's public acceptance seemed to go up, but his Vietnam critics reopened their attacks. As a fairly direct response to these criticisms, on November 13th Mr. Agnew attacked the TV news medium for its lack of objectivity. Again the public response seemed to be more favorable than unfavorable. This time Mr. Agnew's speech counteracted the criticisms of Mr. Nixon's Vietnam policy by questioning the credibility of the TV news medium and by drawing attention away from Vietnam.

Then, moving from a defensive position to an offensive one, on November 20th Mr. Agnew indicted the press news medium. This speech focused attention on the news media and further undermined public confidence in anything the media might say by questioning its objectivity.

So what are the immediate and long-term effects of Mr. Agnew's strategy of diversion in the evolving Nixon administration rhetoric? Initially it has been very effective. It has strengthened the political right by making its rhetoric more dominant—Mr. Agnew echoes the 1964 Republican campaign. This of course is consistent with Mr. Nixon's recent strategy of blocking the movement of public opinion to the left on Vietnam—he is against acceptance

---

Mr. Brock is Associate Professor of Speech, Communication, and Theatre Arts and Director of Forensics at the University of Minnesota.

of rapid disengagement. However, it is most successful as a diversionary tactic, taking attention away from Vietnam and giving the President more time to implement his policy without severe criticism.

The long-term effects are more difficult to assess. It is already clear that the series of speeches have added significantly to the division in society that is already present—we are now also divided over acceptance of the sources of all public information. And by making the attack so personal and emotional, bitterness has resulted from the ensuing charges and counter-charges. One must question what is to be gained by attacking and under-mining public confidence in the mass media. In the past this strategy has not been fruitful—Mr. Nixon in 1962, Mr. Goldwater in 1964, Mr. Romney in 1967, and Mr. Humphrey in 1968.

Mr. Agnew's strategy of using the mass media as a diversionary scapegoat has initially been successful, but in the long run it could backfire. In the current situation with the cities already powder kegs and the youth across the nation quite restless, this is a dangerous strategy. No one can accurately predict how much more pressure the situation can stand before there is an explosion.

STUDENT DISSIDENTS:
STRATEGIC ROLE IN NIXON'S CONSENSUS STYLE

Rebecca Mowe

Richard Nixon's administration has been characterized by a consensus style of leadership which attempts to draw maximum support from a broad range of political ideologies. In a time when the Vietnam War and racial conflict encourage polarity rather than solidarity, it is especially important for a leader who promised to "bring us together" to find some other issue for which he can arouse enthusiastic support and to use such an issue to his advantage. Hugh Dalziel Duncan suggests that a strong unifying force can be found in hatred for a mutual enemy. "Nothing keeps love or friendship alive more than a common enemy. Political bonds, too, are often forged in hatred for a common enemy; . . ."[1] The unifying influence of hatred is a recurring theme of Eric Hoffer's *The True Believer*, with Hitler's exploitation of anti-Semitic feeling being perhaps his most potent historical support. It is the opinion of this writer that Richard Nixon is employing this unifying strategy as part of his leadership style by capitalizing on the unpopularity of a small segment of American society—campus demonstrators. In supporting its thesis, this essay will examine Nixon's strategy to determine why students have become his focus, how the strategy has been implemented, and what might be its implications for future Administration policy.

Stewart Alsop suggests that to qualify for the position of public enemy, a minority must be virtually powerless in terms of voting strength, unanimously opposed to the President, and widely hated by the public.[2] Campus demonstrators in particular and students in general fit this description.

Students are powerless in terms of voting strength, having less than two percent of the voting population. For good measure, they are without economic power, for although they have resources sufficient to make Madison Avenue take note, they do not have the kind of concentrated resources that impress Washington.

Student opposition to Nixon has been made abundantly clear. His own staff reports "total hostility to the Administration among young people—just as strong among those who supported him during the campaign as those who opposed him."[3] And given the direction of Administration policy, there is little hope of bringing the student bloc into the Nixon fold.

The extent to which student protesters are disliked by the general public has become apparent only in the last year. In recent months, Gallup polls have shown that Americans by a five to one margin hold students primarily responsible for the killings at Kent State rather than the National Guard;[4] and Harris pollsters have found that college demonstrators are more gen-

Rebecca Mowe (B.A., University of Oregon, 1969) is a Teaching Associate and M.A. candidate in the Department of Speech, Communication, and Theatre Arts, University of Minnesota.

[1] Hugh Dalziel Duncan, *Symbols in Society* (New York: Oxford University Press, 1968), p. 102.
[2] Stewart Alsop, "Nixon and the Anti-Kid Vote," *Newsweek*, June 15, 1970, p. 112.
[3] *Newsweek*, June 8, 1970, p. 19.
[4] *Newsweek*, May 25, 1970, p. 30.

erally detested than prostitutes, atheists, and homosexuals.[5] The most obvious reason for this hatred is public reaction to tactics of student demonstrators. But a second explanation lies in the failure of American students to conform to the image set for them by the public. As Richard Poirier writes, ". . . youth has ceased to fulfill the 'literary' role which American society has been anxious to assign them."[6] Students are supposed to study, and their natural habitat is the Great University, an institution which embodies all the qualities society imagines itself to possess. When students fail to play their roles, and instead attack the institution, society reacts. Philip Selznick writes,

> No enemy is so dangerous as he who threatens these valued principles and structures . . . the haloed reverenced symbols of public weal, the last bastions which dare not be surrendered, without which life itself seems worthless . . .[7]

Demonstrators have become this enemy, and the American public has responded to the threats to its values with a powerful dislike for students.

Campus demonstrators, then, qualify quite well for duties as black sheep of the national family. They are powerless economically as well as in terms of voting power; they are completely opposed to the Nixon administration and promise to remain so; they are strongly disliked by the very people who form the bulk of Nixon's support.

Students constitute an ideal public enemy. But has the Nixon administration taken advantage of this? The extent to which Nixon has used the scapegoat strategy can be seen in the actions of his administration in dealing with youth, and in public statements to the nation and to young people.

Nixon's actions appear on the surface to be the actions of a leader who wishes to include all dissenting groups in his considerations. He has put his support behind legislation to lower the voting age, arranged meetings with student representatives, and initiated studies on problems of youth. These are conciliatory gestures, attempts to assist students in making their ideas known. But these activities are designed not to accommodate dissent, but rather to give the appearance of accommodation. Support for lowering the voting age has resulted not in a workable Constitutional amendment, but in questionable legislation which faces severe Court tests. Nixon's previous doubts as to the Constitutionality of such legislation have been conveniently ignored. His meetings with student "representatives" exclude those students who disagree strongly with Presidential policies, and these meetings and various commissions are window dressing for an administration that has failed to respond to student dissent. The hours Nixon spends with his showcase commissions do not make up for the hours spent during the post-Cambodia Washington march watching a football game. His actions give only a superficial impression of concern for dissenting student views.

Similarly, many Administration speeches give the impression that Nixon admires and welcomes dissent, while actually alienating students from the Administration and the public from students. Speeches related to student demonstrators and other youth are either conciliatory or inflammatory in nature, although even those which appear to be conciliatory are not intended

---

[5] Alsop, "Anti-Kid Vote," p. 112.
[6] Richard Poirier, "The War Against the Young," *Atlantic*, October, 1968, p. 63.
[7] Philip Selznick, "Institutional Vulnerability in Mass Society," *The American Journal of Sociology*, LVI (1951), p. 329.

to appeal to the demonstrators themselves, but rather to the famed silent majority and the small group of students who are Administration supporters. One such speech was delivered by Nixon at commencement exercises at General Beadle State College in Madison, South Dakota. The student body at Beadle State, not surprisingly, is among the ranks of Nixon supporters. The address was advertised as an answer to campus revolutionaries, but the choice of audience is indicative of the intention of the President to avoid hostilities and serious issues. Not once in the speech did he mention the Vietnam War, the single most important cause of national student dissent, nor did he speak of other sources of dissent. Instead, he delivered a glowing tribute to America, intoning the virtues of liberty, freedom, justice, and human dignity. As he said in previewing the speech, "The challenge I speak of is deeper [than physical confrontation]: the challenge to our values, and to the moral base of authority that sustains those values."[8] His speech was conciliatory in that it raised no issues, but it did not constitute a serious attempt to achieve consensus with American youth. It did achieve two things, however. First, it made the President appear to be a reasonable man, sympathetic to young people, yet fully committed to American values. Second, it implied that these young revolutionaries were exactly the opposite—unreasonable, unthinking, and most important, un-American. The whole speech was a comment *on* dissenters, but not *to* them.

A second "conciliatory" statement was made by the President to another gathering of typical American students in the same week, this time at a Billy Graham crusade on the University of Tennessee campus. Here the President told the students that, "I am proud to say that the great majority of America's young people do not approve of violence. The great majority do approve, as I do, of dissent."[9] In voicing his approval of those students who do not approve of violence, the President is telling the silent majority that although their sons and daughters, the "student majority," are basically good kids, there is another group whose tactics are so undesirable as to isolate them not only from the older generation, but also from the valuable members of their own. In this way, Nixon's rhetoric appeals to the middle American parents who form his power base. One might get the impression from this statement by the President that the group he considers to be undesirable is very small and insignificant. However, he does not consistently distinguish between violent students and the non-violent. The prime example of his failure to isolate violent students from the mainstream on campus is found in his statement following the Kent State incident. Despite the fact those killed and injured were among his "great majority of America's young people" who are non-violent, the President made a sweeping indictment of all present by noting merely that, "when dissent turns to violence, it invites tragedy." It is not difficult to comprehend the harsh attitude of most Americans toward Kent State students when the President himself laid the blame for the killings on the students. The polls on Kent State show the widespread acceptance of Nixon's view and the success of his strategy.

The primary effect of this first group of statements is the enhancement of the President's ethos. He appears very reasonable, very generous, very dignified, very open-minded—in short, everything a president should be. On occasion, he takes the offensive, as at the Air Force Academy, where

[8] Richard M. Nixon, "Campus Revolutionaries," *Vital Speeches*, July 1, 1969, p. 546.

[9] *Time*, June 8, 1969, p. 13.

he condemned those who would have "America turn away from greatness," or as in his June 8 television address in which he decried the "mindless attacks on all the great institutions," and claimed that our "great universities are being systematically destroyed." (Note the implication of conspiracy.) The reference to student "bums" is another example.

But for the most part, the Nixon strategy delegates these unstatesmanlike attacks to the Vice President, who carries much of the President's authority with little of the responsibility. Herb Klein, Administration Director of Communications, explains that Agnew's "assignment is to explain in a missionary way what Administration policies are and to seek support for them. He fills a basic need which a President cannot do."[10] Rhetorically, Agnew fills Nixon's need for an agent to deliver what amounts to a restrained hate message aimed at casting college demonstrators in a scapegoat role. And, as Nixon has said of Agnew, "He has done a great job for this administration." Whether or not Agnew is following specific directions from above is not important, for as John Osborne notes,

> On things that matter, such as "the subtle dangers" posed to the nation by impudent snobs and liberals "who characterize themselves as intellectuals," the President and the Vice President don't need much direct communication. They understand each other perfectly.[11]

This writer must conclude with Jules Witcover, among others, "either that Spiro Agnew is abiding by the wishes or the command of his boss, or that he is a fool."[12]

Giving the Vice President the benefit of the doubt, let us consider the effect of some of his much publicized rhetoric. His most famous attack sent middle America running to its dictionary to search for "masochism," "effete," and "impudent." "Snobs" they understood. And "snobs" they liked, for it reflected the widely held resentment of the young elites who form the core of student dissent. Agnew did not have to create a hatred of student dissenters; he had merely to add the official seal of approval to the intense dislike already present. That he is in great demand as a speaker attests to his ability to tell the silent majority what it wants to hear.

In the same month as his New Orleans speech, Agnew delivered an attack in Harrisburg, Pennsylvania, which was even more explicit in its approval of anti-kid sentiment. Here he stated,

> America cannot afford to write off a whole generation for the decadent thinking of a few. America cannot afford to divide over their demagoguery—or to be deceived by their duplicity—or to let their license destroy liberty. We can afford to separate them from our society—with no more regret than we should feel over discarding rotten apples.[13]

This is perhaps the most clear statement of the Administration's abandonment of a pure consensus style. Agnew is plainly saying that America (and the Administration) can do without such un-American types, will in fact be better off without them. The phrase "separate from our society" clearly places dissidents in the role of social enemy. He even says that they are a

---

[10] *Newsweek,* November 17, 1969, p. 39.

[11] John Osborne, "Spiro Agnew's Mission," *New Republic,* November 15, 1969, p. 20.

[12] Jules Witcover, "Spiro Agnew: The Word's the Thing," *The Progressive,* July, 1970, p. 17.

[13] *Newsweek,* November 17, 1969, p. 38.

divisive force, indicating that national unity would profit from their "separa-
tion." This single paragraph from Agnew's speech summarizes the thrust
of the entire Administration approach to young dissenters; they cannot be
brought into the national base of support, so they must be cut out and
despised.

American youth fill the requirements for a political scapegoat, being, as
a group, without voting power, totally opposed to those in power, and widely
hated. The Nixon administration has taken advantage of this in its consensus
style of leadership by using this hatred of a common enemy to unify its base
of support. Student dissidents have become, in Burke's terms, the rhetorical
agency rather than purpose. This strategy has been implemented in actions
and statements by the President and his vice presidential spokesman.

The analysis is not complete, however, until implications for future
strategies and policies are considered. Up to this point, the national dislike
for youth has been exploited with restraint by the Nixon administration.
Hopefully, this restraint will be continued. But there is every possibility
that the Administration may feel forced to extend the use of the student
scapegoat. Nixon has assumed the role of statesman very successfully, so
successfully that his association with McCarthyism has been virtually forgotten. But there is no guarantee that Administration use of young demonstrators as a unifying force will not extend to the repressive stages, as did
the anti-Communist rhetoric of twenty years ago. Such fears have been
voiced by Alsop,[14] McEvoy and Miller,[15] and Roscoe and Geoffrey Drummond.[16] Murray Chotiner, Nixon advisor in the McCarthy period, master of
the smear campaign, now back in Nixon's inner circle, has commented that
campus unrest is a very good issue to keep in mind for campaign purposes.[17]
Should the Nixon administration get into serious trouble or should the silent
majority be faced with an unacceptable defeat in Southeast Asia, someone
will have to pay, and if present strategy counts for anything, the most likely
candidate is on the American campus. Even now, Agnew's suggestion that
these undesirables be separated from society has the vaguely menacing ring
of repression, as did Hitler's "ultimate solution" of the Jewish problem.
Duncan writes,

> The "perfect" victim is one whose power is so great that we must summon
> all our energy, cunning, skill, luck, and piety, to defeat him, or one so
> beloved that in sacrificing him we give up something of great value.[18]

American youth is both beloved and despised, a combination of feelings
that has made it very vulnerable to the attacks of an administration which
has incorporated it into a consensus style of leadership. Hopefully, this administration will resist the temptation to transform dissenting youth from
black sheep status to sacrificial lamb for the American public.

---

[14] Alsop, "Anti-Kid Vote," p. 112.

[15] James McEvoy and Abraham Miller, *Black Power and Student Rebellion* (Bel-
mont, California: Wadsworth Publishing Company, Inc., 1969), p. 5.

[16] Roscoe and Geoffrey Drummond, "Nixon Could be Tempted," *St. Paul Dis-
patch*, June 19, 1970.

[17] *Ibid.*

[18] Duncan, *Symbols*, p. 146.